SMALL TOWN BIG IMPACT

107 Simple Marketing Strategies for Regional Business Success

Jenn Donovan

To Russ – You're Simply the Best, Better than all the Rest.
Better than Anyone, Anyone I've ever met.
Thank you for being the best other half a girl could wish for.

Alexander, Fletcher and Charlotte, you are my greatest achievements.
I love your stinking guts. I am so glad to be your Mum.

Mum and Dad – thanks for everything, always.

My Jo Jo – thank you. This is because you pushed me to be more.

Michelle – your unwavering support means more than
you will ever know.

First published in 2023 by Jenn Donovan

A catalogue entry for this book is available from the National Library of Australia.

ISBN: 978-1-923007-63-5

Printed in Australia
Book production and text design by Publish Central
Cover design by Julia Kuris

The paper this book is printed on is environmentally friendly.

CONTENTS

Chapter 3: Timeless tactics   65

Chapter 4: The one percenters that can help you be a better marketer 115

Chapter 5: Outside the marketing box thinking 129

Chapter 6: Harder things to do **163**

Chapter 7: The power of email marketing **199**

The future of marketing **214**

Final thoughts **219**

FOREWORD

Okay, it's time to get a little serious about this thing called MARKETING.

My name is Andrew Griffiths, and in one shape or another I've been helping small businesses around the world to grow, to increase their profitability and, most importantly, to become far more financially resilient and strong, through smart marketing, for many years. And that's exactly why I love Jenn Donovan's new book, *Small Town Big Impact*.

For most small business owners, marketing is a mystery. It's complicated and complex, and as technology rapidly evolves, it's easy to get left behind. It's unlikely that marketing is going to get simple anytime soon, hence the need to have the right people and the right resources to help us all navigate these tricky waters. And once again, that's where Jenn Donovan and her new book become so important.

We all need marketing advice that is real – meaning it's actionable, we can implement it without needing a marketing degree and, most importantly, it works. Reading *Small Town Big Impact*, it's crystal clear that the advice offered is smart, practical and proven, and in my opinion, every idea will work if you implement it well. And when you've got 107 strategies, you have everything you need to build a really strong, smart and successful marketing approach for your business.

I like the fact that the advice shared by Jenn Donovan covers both new marketing thinking, specifically digital marketing, as well as more of the old school marketing, or in her words, 'classic marketing'. The key of course with both is to be bold, be creative and be consistent. That's why there are a lot of 'how to', step-by-step instructions throughout the book, and in fact with pretty much every tip, to help you implement the recommended strategies.

Last but not least, the reason it was so easy for me to endorse *Small Town Big Impact* and Jenn Donovan became clear in the first few pages. Jenn talks about her love of marketing, and her passion for marketing, and I know, without a moment of doubt, that if you aren't passionate about marketing your business, it won't work. And if you're going to take advice about marketing your business, you need to take it from someone who is not only extremely capable but also extremely passionate. Tick both boxes for Jenn Donovan.

My advice is simple: follow Jenn's lead. Work through her strategies, and implement them well. Focus on quality over quantity. Get excited as you start to see the results. You're about to embark on a fabulous transformational journey that will have a far-reaching impact on your business and your life.

Enjoy the ride.

Andrew Griffiths

The entrepreneurial futurist

Bestselling author of 14 books

WHERE MY LOVE FOR MARKETING ALL BEGAN ...

I t all began back in 2010, when I decided to sign up for a nine-week business transformation marketing program through my shire. Although I wasn't really sure what it was about or how it would work, I was curious enough that I went along anyway.

I walked into the room, a demountable portable room that felt like a decommissioned classroom from the 1970s, to find a group of local business owners waiting for everyone to arrive. There was a man at the front with funky facial hair, lounging comfortably in the chair, dressed casually but "city" casual, and who had a presence I instantly did not like. In fact, the word I used to describe him to my business partner that afternoon, rhymed with "anchor".

Who was this "city" boy, coming to my country town, telling me how to market my business? What did he know about running a business in the country?

Turns out – a lot. This city boy (or man) changed my life forever.

He set me on a path of loving marketing, a path I am yet to get off, all these years later. And although he didn't know about the difference between marketing a business in the city versus marketing a business in the country, he still had loads to teach me.

Marketing ... probably the nine-letter word small business owners find the most mystifying.

It's a little frustrating that babies and businesses don't actually come with a step-by-step instruction manual. (Until now – for marketing anyway. Babies, I can't do – sorry.)

1

According to The Big Small Business Survey, over 86 percent of small businesses have little to NO marketing plan. And with four out of five small business owners failing in the first five years, according to the Australian Bureau of Statistics, it's no wonder small business owners are finding things tough.

It's worth noting here that in my experience, four out of five businesses DON'T actually fail in the first five years, but the owners are frankly so exhausted from working ridiculous hours for (often) less than minimum wage, they burn out. Their passion for what they started is such a distant memory that the freedom of working for someone else and having a consistent wage is more appealing.

Could marketing their business better, more consistently, more strategically have helped them survive? I think the answer is more than likely, yes. It's a harsh truth and the reason this book exists.

Business owners spend way too much time working IN their business and not ON their business. If they aren't growing it, then it's like a pig driving a truck – it's never going to end well. Survival in business is 80% marketing, 10% passion and 10% good business model.

Actually, if I'm honest, it's 100% about marketing. Marketing is everything. Everything you say and do in your business says something about you and your business, whether you mean it to or not.

Pause here and read that again.

The way you answer the phone says something about you and your business.

The way you write or respond to that email.

The way you post on social media and even what your caption says.

And either fortunately or unfortunately, depending on your glass half full or empty philosophy, in the country it's also the way you show up at the supermarket, at the pub on a Friday night or how you treat the young "after school kid" who serves you at the local fish'n'chip shop.

It's all marketing.

I know you didn't go into business hoping to fail, hoping to be soul-crushed by the end of each day, and I didn't either. In fact, if you're like me, you probably went into business because you wanted freedom, wanted to answer only to yourself and wanted some money to spend when you got the freedom you'd been hoping for.

So, my advice in this book is simple. Really simple. Learn to market your business, so you don't become a statistic.

And it's here that I need to say *congratulations*, because you've got this book – a book on marketing and you've opened it and read to here. That's a good start.

But businesses can only grow one way – with clients (or customers – same/same).

Without them, you have no business.

How do you get more clients or keep the ones you've got? The answer is marketing. In fact, you'll find answers to most questions in these pages will be *marketing*.

I'm sure you are thinking about now – *Jenn, I just don't have time. I have a billion other jobs to do today, not to mention all the stuff I need to do before Monday, I have mouths to feed, staff depending on me, boxes to unpack, emails to send, customers to talk to and frankly, I've tried this marketing "stuff" before and I'm just tired.*

I know.

I do know.

And although I don't know all the challenges you are facing right now in business, I do know my own as a small business owner in the country.

I often think back to my 17-plus years in law and sarcastically laugh at my naivety around business. I sat at my desk and my boss (or in later years, business partner) would slap a file on my desk and that was the new client. I never thought once about where that client came from. Years on, I do know what it takes to get that client. Marketing and lots of it.

Later, I purchased a retail shop with my bestie, and we had zero customers, zero retail experience and frankly, zero idea of what we were doing, with zero marketing experience. But it was here that I found my love for marketing, especially digital marketing.

It was here that I enrolled myself in that business transformation program and never looked back.

After seven years, that retail business went from zero to growth of 11,786% and sold in three days.

That was back in 2017 and since then I've been travelling the country, with a real focus on rural and regional small businesses, delivering workshops, building communities, delivering keynotes and webinars, working one-on-one, and doing countless Zoom calls, where I have impacted almost half a million small businesses. My sole focus has been to see more businesses thrive because they are now focusing on their marketing. I am also a co-founder of the Australian Rural Business Awards, created in 2022 to celebrate all things business in rural and regional Australia.

I've helped hundreds of thousands of small rural and regional business owners through the Facebook group I created, *Buy from a Bush Business,* and through the online marketplace I co-founded www.spendwithus.com.au, which has injected more than eight million dollars back into the Australian country economy.

My weekly podcast, *Small Business Made Simple*, is ranked in the top 1.5% globally, according to Listen Notes and I also write a weekly blog, with both of these things guiding and giving tips to business owners just like you.

Throughout this book I will share not only 107 marketing tips (plus some bonus ones), but I'll share my business journey and loads of stories of other small business owners, just like you, who are using marketing to grow.

Not all the tips will apply to all the businesses. That's actually not the point. The point is to open your eyes to the world of marketing, the breadth and depth of marketing, to make you think differently about how you market your business, how you market you, and how much focus you give this important part of your business.

I want you to be able to open any page of this book, read and choose a tip to implement into your business.

I want your business to be the best business in your town. The one everyone talks about – "Gosh, they are so lucky, look at their amazing business." But we know it's nothing to do with luck – it's strategic, it's planning and it's marketing working the best it can behind the scenes to create the business you dream of, that everyone else can envy.

I want nothing else from you after reading this book except that you are now making time to do marketing. Sectioning out time in your diary to implement a specific, amazing marketing tactic and then sectioning out some more time to measure if it worked.

That's all I want. I hope that as I share my tips, stories, anecdotes and ideas with you that you will be inspired and have your own moments of clarity around business and marketing.

But mostly, I hope that I can make marketing fun. I love marketing – it's the best thing I get to do in a day. It's my sunshine. I hope some of that rubs off on you, too.

How to get the most out of this book

This is my first book (but won't be my last), so I'm writing it in a pretty relaxed and chilled country way. Reading the book from cover to cover is not really what I intended for you – happy for you to do it, but because you're busy, my intention is for you to open any page, read, find a tip that makes you curious, and implement this into your business. Testing and measuring as you go, of course.

Again, not all tips will work for all businesses, but being open to all tips will expand your marketing knowledge. You will no doubt see themes running through the entire book and often I will repeat myself – on purpose for importance and impact – just in case you missed it the first time.

Marketing really isn't hard. Do more stuff to get more clients – do more stuff to keep old clients coming back. Do good stuff.

As you are reading this book, please take a moment to read the quotes at the beginning of each section. These names you probably haven't heard of – yet. These people are people I admire and love and are pivotal to the success I've had or the success I look forward to in the future. Read their names, google them – I promise they will enrich your lives too with their knowledge and amazingness.

Reading this book and running a business are a lot alike. Both take commitment, effort and that precious resource – time. I hope *Small Town Big Impact* becomes your go-to marketing book for many years and when you're feeling stuck, you'll flick open another page for some more Jenn marketing inspiration.

Marketing might have endless possibilities – but let's just start with 107.

Chapter 1

MASTERING THE MARKETING BASICS

Perfection is a trap. There's no such thing as perfect because perfect to you is different from perfect for me. So just start. Don't wait for perfect. It doesn't exist.

Jenn Donovan, author,
Mulwala, NSW

The first 10 tips you are about to read are all about the marketing basics. If you get these right, you are well on your way to being more profitable, having more time and money and making marketing a priority.

Some of the tips are my own business values and philosophies I really wanted to share with you. Some you might have heard before but need to hear again – as Confucius says, *when the student is ready, the teacher appears*. And some might be brand new concepts that simply change your perspective on marketing and business. But all are the basics of business and you need to work through them, work on them and get them right to grow your small country business.

Ready, Fire, Aim – Perfection is a trap

I live my life by a simple philosophy, one that was shared with me many years ago from a business mentor and one that has served me well since. And I suggest you consider adopting it.

Here it is …

Ready, Fire, Aim.

The world doesn't need another amazing small country business owner "aiming" to do something. Aiming to do their marketing, aiming to branch into new markets, aiming to get to know their numbers so they have a better handle on where their business is going or its profitability. No, instead the world needs more ACTION TAKERS.

The secret to getting the business success that you dream of is to become an ACTION TAKER.

To be an action taker you need to be more interested in producing results than perfection. Perfection is the killer of action.

I would not have started my podcast, *Small Business Made Simple* (ranked in the top 1.5% of podcasts globally according to Listen Notes),

> **To be an action taker you need to be more interested in producing results than perfection. Perfection is the killer of action.**

if I hadn't been an action taker. If I had waited around to do a course on how to podcast or decided that I couldn't launch until I had a concrete plan, all the equipment that I needed and everything was perfect, then I probably would never have launched it. Instead, I watched a few YouTube videos, purchased what I thought looked like a good mic, wrote a list of subjects I could talk about (there were 27) and I started. I got READY and then I FIRED. I took aim at perfection and honing my craft as I went.

My business life is full of stories just like this. I was terrified of public speaking but wanted to step outside my comfort zone, so I enrolled in a professional speaking course. I'd never run a business retreat by myself before, but deployed my Ready, Fire, Aim philosophy and pulled it off – everyone loved it. I didn't know how to use Canva (a graphic design program) but learnt it. Hated Instagram, but knew that was where my audience was hanging out, so found out all I could about Instagram. I watched videos, followed the right people, tested and measured results for myself and learned all I could. And I'm still learning, because change happens quickly.

Why did I take action? Because the success of my business depended on it. If I wanted to stand out from my competitors and stand out from the crowd, I needed to do a podcast and make it the best marketing podcast in the country. If I wanted to be good at social media and help others, I had to go first, learn, test, measure, make the mistakes so I could be a better mentor. Without these and many more actions, my business would either be dead or I would be miserable attracting all the wrong clients to my business.

To get the most out of this book, you need to be an action taker. As I said in the introduction, if you don't take action, then this has been just a good book to read.

Instead of aiming for perfection and waiting for the perfect moment to make that important call, book a meeting or create a marketing piece, read the amazing marketing book in your hands, just take the leap and FIRE. The only time you ever really have is now. Your business results rely on the decisions you make now. If you want a brighter future, it's today's decisions that will get you there.

Marketing is everything

As I mentioned in my introduction, marketing is *everything*.

Everything you *do* and everything you *say* in business says something about you, regardless of whether you mean it to or not.

So, I could literally finish the book here – marketing is everything – done. But I feel we need to go just a wee bit deeper.

People do business with people they know, like and trust. How do they discover if they know, like and trust you? By watching – watching from the sidelines.

Marketing is everything. But don't let that scare you. Embrace it.

Make marketing a priority

Why does it need to be a priority? The answer is simple. If you want to grow, you need to learn to put the right message in front of the right audience, at the right time so that they will buy what you sell. And then (this is the kicker), they will not only come back again and again as repeat customers but also be a referrer of business to you and become your biggest fan.

If you want to grow, you have to market. If no-one knows about you, what you sell or why they should buy from you rather than everyone else who sells what you sell, then you will fail in business. Marketing is the key to meeting your financial goals.

Know who your who is

Who is your who, who is your ideal client or ideal client avatar? I'm sure if you've been in business for any amount of time, you have heard these expressions. It's basically working out who your buyer is. If you could wish for one person, one type of person to be your buyer, to make your business profitable and successful, who would it be?

Because, news flash – **not everyone is your client or customer**. I know lots of business owners who are afraid to market to a niche

" Everything you *do* and
everything you *say* in
business says something
about you, regardless of
whether you mean it
to or not. "

group at the exclusion of others, thinking that they are missing out on money from the groups they aren't targeting.

I absolutely guarantee you that if you target your marketing to a niche group – then your business will grow more quickly and will be more profitable than if you spray and pray targeting everyone with everything.

Pepsi toppled Coke in the 80s by focusing on one small section of the population and they've been competitive ever since. They niched down, marketed to that group, and the marketing worked not only for the target market but created what we now refer to FOMO – Fear Of Missing Out. The people in the target group were in their 20s and 30s but those over 30 were like, "Hey, we're cool and hip too, we want to buy it." Those under the targeted group thought they were grown up enough to be involved as well.

Just because you target a certain section of the market to the exclusion of others, doesn't mean the others aren't going to come and be buyers anyway. FOMO – it's a great marketing strategy too.

So many small business owners don't understand their ideal client; they don't understand the power of knowing their ideal client. Their business never grows because they don't know who they serve and therefore how to market to them to attract them. Please don't be this business owner.

> **CHALLENGE**
>
> I have put together the Ideal Client Avatar Workbook to help you identify your idea client. Put aside an hour this week, download the workbook and get stuck into it – https://bit.ly/ICAJenn. [Don't stress too much about remembering these URLs – there's a QR code at the back of the book with this all listed. Scan that when you're ready].

Where does your ideal client hang out?

Do you know where your ideal client hangs out? Do you know where to market to them? Do they read the papers or magazines, do they live in their inboxes reading emails, are they in LinkedIn groups or Facebook groups or on Instagram? Maybe they are Twitter (now known as X) people or avid podcast listeners.

Marketing is simple (not easy, but simple) when you know where to market. Wherever they are, be there, participate there, give enormous free value there so that they are so curious they click, download, start following you, come into your store or request to connect.

This book is all about helping you find the best way to market to them – there's 107 tips after all in this book. But if you don't know WHERE to test, measure, polish, and test again these marketing tips, then they simply will never work because your audience isn't there to see you marketing to them.

In the digital age of marketing, there are tonnes of places to market to your ideal client and there's always another way coming.

In my Facebook group, Like Minded Business Owners (go join that if you haven't already), someone mentioned Tik Tok not so long ago. The question was – do you use Tik Tok in your business? The response was – oh no, not another thing I need to be doing. It's a valid point, right? We are all busy enough – do we need another thing?

There are a lot of platforms you COULD be on, there are a lot of places you could market to your ideal client – but which ones SHOULD you?

The short answer is – where your audience is. Did you see that one coming?! But it makes logical sense, yes?

We aren't on social media or sending emails or making podcasts for fun (not really). We are using them as tools to attract an audience, to nurture an audience until they are ready to buy. Then we are using these tools to enable our audience to discover why we are the right fit for them to come back and buy again and tell their friends about us and our products or services.

So, if you want more sales, you need to get in front of more potential buyers. It comes back to knowing who your ideal client is – your ideal audience, your avatar – whatever you want to call them.

Who's your target audience, the audience that is most likely to buy your stuff? Where do they hang out? Get these two questions right and no matter how many times someone talks about Tik Tok or Instagram or LinkedIn or email marketing or whatever, you know you do or don't need to be on those platforms, because you know where your audience is hanging out.

Let's look at some examples of an ideal client.

Benny Boy

First up, let me introduce you to Benny Boy. He:

- is 25 years old, and already a serial entrepreneur
- is single with a high five-figure salary
- graduated with a double degree from Melbourne University
- is from Gen Z
- wants to make $$ but also an impact on the world
- is a busy guy with a great social life
- embraces all sorts of new tech – loves having the latest gadgets
- loves the outdoors and adventure.

Given all this information, where would you potentially market to Benny Boy? It could be:

- the latest social media platforms like TikTok
- LinkedIn
- SMS marketing
- Quora
- Reddit
- paid digital marketing such as Facebook/Instagram ads
- Google Ads
- Google (organic)
- networking events
- SnapChat.

Where wouldn't you market to Benny Boy? It wouldn't be:

- radio
- Spotify (he'd pay for premium, he's not that tight)
- Instagram Reels – dancing and singing
- print media
- email.

Obviously, I am assuming a lot about Benny Boy but that's kind of the point – you need to make assumptions about your ideal (fictional) avatar – test, measure, fix, polish, repeat.

Is your ideal client Benny Boy or someone similar? If yes, are you marketing to him in the right places?

Mary Contrary

Next, we have Mary Contrary. This is what we know about Mary Contrary. She:

- loves social media – follows loads of influencers
- works part-time and runs a side hustle from home that brings in a modest five-figure income
- has a law degree she no longer uses
- has two children
- her partner is the main breadwinner
- millennial (33 years old) – and ready to change the world
- fit, healthy and values both qualities
- always busy doing something and always has her phone nearby.

So where would you potentially market to Mary Contrary? It could be:

- TikTok
- Instagram – everywhere – reels, stories, lives
- Facebook groups
- Quora
- Reddit
- paid digital marketing such as Facebook/Instagram ads
- Google Ads
- Google (organic)
- networking events
- online blogs/magazines
- email.

And where won't you market to Mary Contrary? It wouldn't be:

- radio
- Spotify (again, she would have premium)
- print media, except perhaps fitness magazines.

Is your ideal client Mary Contrary or someone similar? If yes, are you marketing to her in the right places?

Lastly, let me introduce you to Eddie not Ready – I have to say, I love Eddie Not Ready.

Eddie not Ready

So, here's what you need to know about Eddie not Ready. He:

- hates technology – would rather not own a smartphone but does under sufferance
- prides himself on not having any social media profiles, as well as buying local at least 96% of the time – he hates online shopping
- Gen X (52 years old), dad of four
- has been a loyal employee to the same company for 24 years and earns 140K a year (yet has no formal education – just loyal and climbed the corporate ladder)
- plays local sport, belongs to Lions Club and enjoys spending Sunday catching up on the news.

He's different to market to, yes? So where would you potentially market to him? It could be:

- local radio
- newspapers
- email marketing
- community boards
- Medium (an online publishing platform)
- shop windows – flyers
- print catalogues
- paid Digital – targeting Messenger (his family makes him have Messenger)
- print media

- Spotify (he's too tight to buy premium)
- Google.

Where would you NOT market to Eddie not Ready? It wouldn't be:

- social media
- Google shopping.

If you are spending all your marketing time and energy on social media, and Eddie not Ready is your ideal client – then I have just poked a hole in your entire marketing strategy. Eddie is not there to market to as he doesn't do social media or look at buying online (google shopping).

But so many small businesses are only doing social media – that's pretty much ALL their marketing plan has in it. They are saying, "I don't really care who my ideal client is. Social media is free and it's what everyone else seems to be doing so I am doing it anyway – even if my client/customer might not be on the platform." Seems rather ridiculous, doesn't it?

CHALLENGE

Take some time out to think WHO is your WHO and where do they hang out – and are you marketing to them on that platform?

It is super important to get the basics correct. So please section out an hour or so this week to take a deep dive on who your who is. Here's the link to my workbook on Ideal Clients – https://bit.ly/ICAJenn. (Or again, see QR code at the end of the book.)

Have a marketing strategy

I'll talk a lot in this book about the importance of having a marketing strategy. All the marketing you do should help you achieve your goals in business. If your marketing is not helping you reach your goals, then you either need new goals or new marketing activities.

The following table breaks marketing down into five strategies.

Type of strategy	Content creation purpose
Engagement	to get engagement from your audience
Brand awareness	to build brand awareness for your business
Growth	to get sales or growth in list building numbers and social following
Lead generation	to gather more leads – get more people into your funnel and into your world to nurture them until they are ready to buy
Sales	to get sales

Do an audit of your content. Look at your recent marketing and decide which of the five categories above it falls into. Start to see patterns of what you are doing and what you are not doing. Are you selling too much, are you never selling? Are you doing nothing to gather leads and build your database?

Once you have done your audit, which one or ones from the five strategies in the table above are being neglected the most and which ones are you doing too much of?

Boosting the five strategies

Let's go through some ideas of what you can do if you are lagging in one area.

If engagement is lacking in your marketing, use more:

- calls-to-action in your marketing
- sharing of relative news (curated content)
- polls, tips, tricks, and sharing of your knowledge.

If brand awareness is lacking in your marketing:

- use storytelling as a marketing tactic
- share reviews and testimonials
- share your business values
- use your reach out strategy wisely and strategically – read more about having a reach out strategy in Tip #21.

If lead generation is lacking in your marketing:

- write blog posts
- create more offers
- speak on a podcast
- create a lead magnet or market the fact that you have one.

If you are lacking in growth strategy, try to:

- share more reviews and testimonials
- create content to generate conversation, leads and community
- implement a reach out strategy
- look for opportunities for connections, collaborations or partnerships.

If your marketing content is lacking in sales strategy, then:

- have more or better calls-to-action in your marketing
- market your products, services or offers more frequently and consistently
- create packages
- follow up leads – oh please, do this one
- have a reach out strategy and do it consistently.

According to the Big Small Business Survey, over 86% of small business owners do not have a comprehensive marketing/business plan. The job of this book is to help create one. Marketing isn't easy, it does take work to build a business, a successful one anyway, but marketing should be simple or at least simpler – which is the reason for writing this entire book, not just this chapter. Let's do this – let's make marketing a priority by making it simpler with a strategy.

The pros and cons of outsourcing your marketing

This is a question I get asked a lot. When you own your own business, there's loads to do every single day and although I talk about making marketing a priority, the reality is that when you're busy being busy inside the business, doing marketing is often last on the list. Hence the question, "Can I outsource my marketing?"

The answer is yes and no. Yes, you can outsource your marketing and no, you probably shouldn't – or at least not until you have a good handle on your marketing yourself.

Outsourcing your marketing – before you understand your own marketing, your customer, marketing channels or what you want to be famous for – is how you achieve mediocre results or don't receive the return on investment you need or are expecting. It is, frankly, how people get ripped off.

If you have no idea who your ideal client is, where they hang out, or what you want to be known for, then how can you expect an outsider, the person you are handing over your marketing to, to know either?

Successful outsourcing of your marketing comes when you out-source to the right person (obviously) and you can give solid direction to that person around who, what, why, where and how. And you have a plan, a strategic marketing plan, to share with them.

Although outsourcing seems like the perfect solution for someone who doesn't have time to do their own marketing, it won't help if you don't have a strategy (fancy word for a plan) for your marketing. If you have a plan, or the person you are outsourcing to can help you reach your goals, this could be a great investment in your business.

My advice with outsourcing is to test and measure. Don't go all in and sign a 12-month contract with someone – make sure they are a good fit for you and that they align with your branding and, in particu-lar, your brand's tone and your business values.

You absolutely get what you pay for. If you want someone to do three posts on social media a week for $50 – you'll get what you paid for. And it won't be good. With posts taking around 30 minutes or more each to create, build assets for, write engaging copy, research, upload and schedule – and you are only paying around $17 per hour – you will get the quality of $17 per hour. The hourly rate I currently pay is much, much higher – around $50-80 per hour. Just think about the difference in not only quality but ROI (return on investment). This is your brand you are putting out there – you want it to be represented in the best possible way.

Start with the end in mind

This tip contains my best piece of business advice. Start with the end in mind. Know the goal – without a goal, how do you know it worked?

When you head to the grocery store, you probably have either a written list of things you need or a list in your head. You may be thinking – I need to cook Monday, Tuesday and Thursday, Wednesday is a meeting so no cooking and Friday is takeaway pizza night. So you go to the supermarket knowing you need to buy meals for three nights – that's your goal. You started with the end in mind. Starting with the end in mind is a concept we use every day in our lives, but many small business owners have a really bad habit of forgetting about it when it comes to business.

Start with the end in mind is a business philosophy of mine, one that I always had, but just didn't know it.

Four days into my business with my best friend, we held our first partners meeting. We'd purchased a rundown retail business with no experience, no customers and no idea what we were doing.

But over a counter-meal at the local pub (also known as our first partners meeting), we agreed wholeheartedly that retail wasn't our thing – this was not our forever job – and we agreed we'd do it for seven years and then sell. Why seven years? I couldn't actually tell you why exactly, but I suspect the seven-year itch theory had something to do with it, perhaps.

It was the best decision we ever made. Literally for the following seven years, everything we did we did with this in mind – to sell in seven years. Thinking about getting a new product line in? Would it help us sell the business? Ad in the local newspaper – would it help us sell the business? Moving to a different location (which we did twice) – would it help us sell the business? You get the point.

Everything we did, we did with this in mind – the end goal – to sell. And we did sell our business six and a half years later, and we sold it in three days. I know that this was made possible almost entirely because we had been working towards this since about day five of owning the business.

You might not have this goal or ever want to sell, and that's totally okay, but you still should have the end in mind and set goals. If your goal isn't to sell, then what is the goal? Are you using your goal to position your business decisions? Let's bring it back to marketing, because it's a marketing book after all.

Let's just say you are investing $20 a day in an ad through Meta. You've spent time and energy working out your audience (target market), their behaviours, interests, location, age demographic and so forth. You've set your budget, worked out the placement of the ad – for example, Instagram stories, Facebook feed and Messenger, and voila your ad is published and beginning to give you some data.

But what's the goal of the ad? If you went deep into the detail (as above) but forgot to set the goal, forgot to start with the end in mind, then how on earth do you know if your money was well spent or not? Without a goal, there's no measure of success, you've got no idea what return you got for that investment.

Your goal might be, for example, I want to make $200 in sales each day from this ad or I want to build my email list by 100 people during the time this ad runs.

Just by setting that intention, that goal, just by starting with the end in mind, all of a sudden we have something to measure success against.

I cannot emphasise enough how important it is to start with the end in mind when you are in business. It filters through all of your business, even down to hiring staff or getting a partner or looking for sponsorship.

This simple sentence – start with the end in mind – could be the five words in this whole book that make a massive difference in your marketing.

The secret of why you lose customers

Why do customers stop buying from you?

This is such a great question. Can I just tell you, straight up, the answer is NOT what you think it is? Most people think it's price.

But very few customers will stop buying from you because of price.

The reasons customers leave

In fact, according to the Rockefeller Corporation (via *Smashing Magazine*), these are the reasons customers leave:

- 1% leave because they are dead – no arguing with that
- 3% of your customers will leave because they have moved away
- 5% stop buying from you because of a recommendation by a friend to a new seller
- 9% of customers are persuaded by competitors to come and shop with them. Yes, just a tiny 9%
- 14% of customers will leave because they are dissatisfied with your service. So customer service is important, but it isn't the major reason why people leave.

And drum roll…

- 68% of customers leave because the customer believes you don't care about them. They think you don't care whether they shop with you or someone else, that their loyalty means nothing to you.

So, how do you stop this hemorrhage of customers and make your customers feel valued, love, treasured, important? Try the following ideas:

- Stop focusing on numbers, followers and likes, and start building a community. Customers come for the content (what you are selling) but they stay for the community.
- Start getting to know your customers by name and building rapport by asking simple questions like, "How's the family?", "Any plans for the weekend?", "How'd Jonny go in that interleague footy match?"
- Create a loyalty program – refer to Tip #37.
- Keep tabs on your customers' happiness – take their happiness temperature every now and then. How? Call them on the phone and ask them how satisfied they are with your service and if they have any suggestions or feedback. Or send them a "How likely are you to recommend us to a friend?" survey where they pick from *not at all likely* to *extremely likely*. More importantly, take action on what you find out from the questions and surveys, because remember, nothing changes if nothing changes.

It doesn't take much to make a customer feel loved, welcomed and treasured in your business. It is really about being a good person who cares about the people who spend their hard-earned money at your business.

If you could stop the bleed of 68% of customers thinking you don't care about them, imagine what that could do for your bottom line.

Make data-driven decisions

Marketing should be based on data, not algorithms. The reason I love digital marketing so much is because the data that we get from our activities can help us build our businesses so much more quickly and accurately.

Old-fashioned marketing strategies, such as advertising in your local newspaper, cannot give you the accurate data that a digital marketing activity can. Yes, the local paper can tell you that your ad will be printed in 1800 papers and distributed to 1500 households all with an average of three people in that household. But it can't tell you how many people actually saw your ad, nor can it tell you how many people took an action because they did see your ad. Results are full of averages and guesswork.

But a paid Facebook ad, for example, can tell you accurately how many people it reached, how many people clicked a link to your website. Then your Google analytics can tell you how long a lead stayed on your website page for, potentially where they scrolled to, if they clicked the "buy now" link and if they did purchase the product you were advertising in the paid Facebook ad. The data is not 100% accurate, because you are dealing with busy humans who click your link and get distracted and might come back five days later to the tab they have saved on their phone or computer, but it is accurate.

Too many business owners I work with use Instagram when it comes to doing their marketing, but the reality is that Instagram brings very few sales and very few leads or traffic to your website. In essence, they are marketing in the wrong place to get sales. We know this because we look at the data and Instagram just doesn't stack up. We look at their Google analytics, and check where their traffic has come from and Instagram either isn't there or is third behind organic traffic and Facebook (just for instance).

So, if you are trying to use social media and are getting frustrated with your lack of traction, sales or leads, or you are sending out emails and need to get a better open rate and click through rate, then look at your data because the answers are staring you in the face. Get some clarity on what's working and what's not, and make some strategic decisions based on what you find. Taking action, as with all marketing, is the key. Digital marketing is making your business life easier – if you can learn to read it and adapt what it's telling you into your strategy.

***

As you read through this book, you will see me referring back to the tips you've just read. Why? Because, like I said at the beginning of this chapter, getting these marketing basics right, getting your mindset right (Ready, Fire, Aim or start with the end in mind) will not only help you be a better marketer, but a better business owner too.

The success of so many small business owners lives and dies in Chapter 1 – the basics. If they don't get these right, all the tips in the rest of the book simply won't work because they are going to put the wrong message in front of the audience at the wrong time.

Marketing isn't easy, but it is simple if you get the basics right from today. Give yourself time to re-read the tips above if you have to, work through the workbook and build the business of your dreams, earn what you are worth and then you can make a bigger difference in your amazing local community.

Chapter 2
SOCIAL MEDIA

Surround yourself
with the type of people
who will mention your
name in a room full of
opportunities.

—

**Jules Brooke, She's the Boss,
Melbourne, Victoria**

You'd think as a marketing and social media strategist, this chapter would have been the first I would write. But it's placed here because we needed a gentle warm-up before we tackled the big, big topic of social media. For small business owners these days, social media makes up so much of the marketing we do. I am not advocating for that, but it is the reality.

When I ask a small business owner what marketing they do, the first words out of their mouth (and sometimes the ONLY words out of their mouth), are Facebook or Instagram or social media. I love that so many have embraced social media, but there's still a lot of marketing to be done or that could be done, aside from social media.

But alas, social media is the necessary evil of business. Frankly if you aren't on social media, your community might wonder if you still exist. Facebook is like the old-fashioned White Pages – you just have to be listed and have a current profile. Instagram and TikTok are required to reach the audience that is no longer on Facebook. My kids and their friends are on social media platforms that I haven't even heard of (and probably never will, due simply to my age!). Then, of course, there's platforms like LinkedIn, Threads and Twitter (or as it's known now, X) that have a different purpose and a different audience again.

So, the following tips under the umbrella of social media are to help navigate this confusing landscape, simplify it for you and give you clarity and direction on which platforms and which features of that platform you should be using. It's no longer which platform should you be using, but which feature of that platform – video (live, long or short), photos, just words, stories, reels and the list goes on.

If you know me at all, you could probably guess where I will start when it comes to marketing strategies to use on social media. It's the number one thing everyone who knows what works on social media talks about and yet it's the one most find the hardest to embrace. Hazard a guess? Yep, you probably got it, let's start this chapter talking about video.

Embrace the power of video

Ask any marketing or business coach what's the best way to get traction on social media and the answer will be video. And if it's not, it should be. We have been told by the platform makers and designers that video is king. Want more reach? Do more video. Want more engagement? Do more video. Want more algorithm? Do more video. Too busy to do marketing? Do more video. You might not like the answer, but when it comes to social media the answer is almost always – do more video.

Of course, the platform you are using will determine which video works best – live or pre-recorded. It will also determine the length of video you should create – 15 seconds, 1 minute, 4 minutes, however long you like – the list goes on.

Why is video king on social media? There are several reasons, one is that it often gets more reach, likes and engagement than "still" posts and that is often because the algorithm likes video, because it thinks we, the humans using social media, like video so it pushes it further into more people's feeds. Of course, a platform like TikTok is all video – if you're on that, there is simply no choice but to create more and more video content. The other reason comes down to what I have been messaging throughout this whole book – human to human marketing. People do business with people they know, like and trust. And how do you build know, like and trust quickly? Video, of course.

Videos are also highly shareable on social media platforms. Users are more likely to share videos they find entertaining, informative or inspiring with their own followers and friends, extending the reach of your content and increasing brand awareness. My messenger groups are full of shared videos on a daily basis.

Videos can take various formats on social media, including tutorials, behind-the-scenes footage, interviews, live streams, animations and more. And because there is so much choice, it is important to find the type of video that resonates best with your community or target audience.

Video might be king, but there are still some rules that need to be followed when creating video for social media. Their success and effectiveness depends on the following factors:

- **Content quality** – this can include the quality of the actual content, what you are saying, but also the sound and video quality.
- **Relevance** – this is the relevance of the messaging to your community.
- **Understanding your target audience** – do they watch video? If so, with sound on or off? Sound off – you'll need captions on all your videos (a great idea regardless).
- **Length of video** – what works best? To answer that question, I'd really need to know your audience. If they are like my audience, busy business owners who don't have enough time in their days, then under three minutes for most videos on social media. The exception is possibly being live video, especially if you are doing a workshop, webinar or a Q&A session.
- **The platform you put the video on** – where your audience is!

CHALLENGE

We all have a camera in our pocket – so pull it out and record a video. Write the script or simply look into the camera and tell your audience something you know would make their life simpler. You don't have to post it anywhere, you don't have to send it to anyone – but you do have to START.

If you're not keen on video at all because of how you think people will look at you – let me tell you two little secrets that will help.

What other people think of you is none of your business – so stop using this excuse – just do it.

The way you sound and look on video is the way you show up every day to the people in your world. Your looks and voice are nothing new to them – just to you because we're not used to seeing and hearing ourselves.

Mastering social media posts

This is where we all started. Long before we had so many choices of things to do on social media, we put up a post. If you've been on social media as long as I have, it used to be brilliant! The simple act of putting up a post used to bring in sales, leads and enquiries. Now, not so much. The reality for most of us is that a post on social media is part of our marketing, not our entire marketing.

Basic social media posting rules to follow

- Start with the end in mind – what do you want your audience to do after they read or watch this post? What's the point of it? The purpose of 99% of content is to education, entertain, inspire or convert.

- Have an attention-grabbing headline. You want people to stop, read and engage with your post.

- Or you'll need an attention-grabbing photo or video. The first three seconds are the most important.

- Always, and I mean always, have a call-to-action in your post. Whether that call to action is "like this post" or "comment below" or "buy now" or somewhere in between, always have an action for your reader to be encouraged to do.

- Be consistent with your brand voice, tone and identity across all social media posts. Incorporate your logo, brand colors and visual style to create a cohesive and recognisable presence. This helps in building brand recognition and loyalty among your audience.

- If the platform you are posting on is one that encourages hashtags, think about what hashtags you will use for the post. Use relevant hashtags to increase the discoverability of your post. Research popular and trending hashtags related to your content and industry. Incorporate them strategically to reach a wider audience and increase engagement.

- Don't just put three words with every post – that's not engaging. Give your readers or watchers a reason to linger a while.

- Use bullet points, subheadings or line breaks to make your content scannable and easy to read, especially if you consider your audience to be busy people – you want to make it simple for them to consume. Make sure you consider the character limits and recommended image sizes for each platform to optimise your posts for better visibility.

- Don't be afraid to mix up your social media posts with wisdom, quotes, asking questions, inviting opinions, running polls, tips, tricks, how to's and many, many more ideas for the humble social media post.

- Don't post and ghost – respond to comments and messages.

- Track the performance of your posts using analytics tools provided by social media platforms.

The benefits of stories

The use of stories here is referring to the popular feature on social media platforms such as Instagram and Facebook, but they are also featured on platforms like Snapchat, WhatsApp, Messenger and YouTube.

Stories provide a more informal and ephemeral way to share moments, updates, behind-the-scenes glimpses, product promotions or any content that you want to showcase in a more temporary and engaging format. They offer a great opportunity to connect with your audience, foster engagement and keep your followers updated on a daily basis.

Instagram stories, for example, are a collection of photos, videos and other content that you can share with your followers. Unlike regular posts that remain on your profile indefinitely, stories are temporary and disappear after 24 hours. They are displayed at the top of the Instagram app in a separate section and are shown in a slideshow format.

Stats tell us, at the time of writing this book, that stories receive higher engagement and views compared to normal "feed posts".

Of course, you need to know your audience to know if they fall into this category or not.

If you hate being on video, stories are a great way to get started, after all they disappear after 24 hours! But they also offer fabulous interactive elements such as polls, questions, quizzes and stickers to catch people's attention as they scroll through. If one of the brands you follow on Instagram, for example, is live on the platform when you are there scrolling, they will appear at the beginning of your stories feed – a great way to capture people's attention when you are going live.

The rules for stories are less so than for posts, as mentioned above. They are more about providing a more relaxed and informal way of sharing content compared to the curated and polished posts on the feed. Users often share behind-the-scenes moments, real-time updates and candid glimpses into their lives through stories, which can be more appealing and relatable.

So, why create content that is going to disappear after 24 hours? So you can show up for your community in a less polished, more real "this is my life" way, and because stories create the FOMO effect (Fear Of Missing Out), there is a sense of urgency among users to view them before they vanish. This creates the fear of missing out on content, encouraging users to check stories more frequently.

And just FYI, on Instagram – they don't really disappear for you as the creator – just for the people looking. You can find all past stories by going to Your Activity in your Instagram menu, and then Archived content. They are all still there!

And also, on Instagram you can make them into highlights. Highlights are those round circles that you can see under your profile bio. You can save stories into different highlights to have them live on. More about highlights later.

Boosting engagement with reels

What is a reel? It's a video form feature that is available on platforms such as Instagram and Facebook and of course, TikTok (although they're not called reels on TikTok – they are just videos).

Reels and similar short-form video features are continually evolving and may be expanded to other platforms in the future. As social media platforms adapt and innovate, new features and functionalities are always being added.

But reels right now are pretty popular, especially on a platform like Instagram – with Facebook definitely encouraging them more with a positive algorithm push. Over 140 billion (yes, that's billion) reels play across Instagram each day according to Instagram themselves. Reels are there to help you grow your community, hop on trends and collaborate with others.

According to Instagram they are the number one media platform for discovering new brands. They are certainly entertaining and are a great media for storytelling.

If you've never done a reel before on Instagram, then templates are a great way to begin. Templates allow you to borrow someone else's structure from their reels – so think Canva template but it's a reels template!

Creating a reel that your audience will engage with is like any other piece of marketing. You need to open with a strong hook in the first five seconds that encourages your viewer to watch to the end, because that matters for algorithm love. And you need a call-to-action at the end.

Jumping on trends is one of the best ways to get reach for your reel. You can find out what's trending by going to Instagram's Reels Trend Report here: https://creators.instagram.com/blog or remix a trending reel that someone else has already done.

How long are reels? This is ever changing. But at this point any video shared on Instagram is shared automatically as a reel but reels under 90 seconds are the sweet spot because they are eligible for being recommended and seen by more people.

Reels are always video format but you can create reels by putting a series of photos together and creating a video from them. This can make it less daunting for you if you're not great at video creation or just need to start somewhere.

But here's my two cents worth of opinion, because no-one asked. Reels are great for reach but not great for sales. They are great for reach but not good for engagement. The way I watch reels and the way millions of others watch reels is by scrolling from one to the other, being delightfully entertained along the way. But to stop, comment, double-tap, like on a reel, or to click through from the reel's feed to an account's bio to find out more is rare – very rare. Therefore, if you're looking for reach, and use reels as part of your brand awareness strategy, then it will probably produce results for you – reach results. But if you are thinking of using reels as part of your sales strategy, you may be disappointed. Also, be very aware of the time you are spending creating reels versus the return on that investment of time.

Go live on social media with others

If the thought of going live on social media gives you the cold sweats, then this marketing strategy is definitely for you. Find a friend and go live with them. If you can't find a friend to go live with – heck, hit me up, I'll go live with you. Anything to get you over the fear of live video.

Live is the ultimate in video. It gets the most algorithm love and you get to interact with your audience live, as long as they are online at the same time, of course.

But let's just say you are comfortable with going live – then let's talk strategy. There are two ways to think about strategy when it comes to going live with others on social media. One, choose someone who is not a direct competitor but has the same audience demographics as you, and potentially has people in their audience that you don't normally get to reach or chat to. This way, you are growing your community and potentially so is the person you are going live with. Two, ensure your conversation in the live is compelling to listen to and have a really strong call to action. Set the goal for the live – what do you want out of it and what do you want the people watching live and on replay to do after they have watched it? It can't be nothing – you need to be more strategic than that.

Your call to action might be as simple as "follow me" or "connect here" or "go to my website" or it can be a little stronger (preferably) and more like "buy this product here" or "download my 108 Social Media Content Creation Ideas" or "subscribe to my monthly roundup newsletter" – a call to action that is collecting data or making sales is always the best action to ask your viewer to take.

You can go live with someone else on just about all platforms. You can either hop online live yourself and invite them on, so then you are live together, or you can use third party apps like Zoom or Streamyard.

Remember to tell your audience that you are going live with your collaboration partner. Send out some emails to say, "Join me live next Monday with Michelle Clark from Judds, here's the link." Use your social media platforms to promote the fact that you are going live at a particular time with that person – the more people you tell you are going live, the more people who will turn up to watch it! If you and the person you are going live with collaborate on some marketing together beforehand, the live will be a success.

Final words – don't get too hung up on how many people were there to watch you live. The reality is that many more will watch the replay, so don't stress if only a few turn up for the live. The content will continue to get reach long after the live finishes.

CHALLENGE

So, who will you choose to go live with? My challenge, as you finish this chapter, is to put the book down now and reach out to three amazing people who have your community, who you can ask if they would do a live with you. Book it in and get it done. The first one is always the hardest. PS – extra points if you tag me into the live or the marketing for the live, I would love to see you making marketing a priority.

Unlocking potential with Facebook Marketplace

Marketplace is specifically tied to Facebook and is usually where you find people advertising their garage sales, secondhand goods, cars for sale and more. If you are a product-based business, have you ever thought about putting your products on Facebook Marketplace with a link back to your website?

A furniture store local to me has taken their business from almost ready to close to financially viable and expanding, using Facebook Marketplace as a marketing tool to sell their furniture, among other strategies. They started using it to get rid of 'last of the best sellers' or products that they would normally sell through a scratch and dent sale – new products that are slightly damaged or solid. But after amazing success, they started putting their everyday range there, even if not on sale.

One thing to watch for is scams. If you are on Marketplace and watch what's on there, you will notice loads of scams. We have purchased all three of my kids' cars over Marketplace and it was definitely an eye-opener for scams – gosh, there were plenty. So, you need to have your wits about you.

If you decided to give Marketplace a try to sell your products, I would recommend you always send customers to your website to complete the purchase. If you don't have an e-commerce platform and you need them to come in and buy the product from your store, then that's the rule – if they want it, they have to come in and get it and pay for it. Don't sway from that rule. If they want to pay via bank deposit and have you send it – say no, your rule is your rule. Of course, this doesn't apply if you know the customer. Please be aware scammers are super clever and this is their job, as tragic as that is – their job is to build up your trust and scam you out of money or product.

I don't say that to scare you from trialling Marketplace as a potential marketing strategy for selling products in your business, but I do want to be real with you. I think it is worth experimenting with, especially if sales are a little slow and you need to reach more people and do something a little different as far as marketing goes. If you have an e-commerce store, then the risk is lower.

Think of using a platform like Facebook Marketplace as putting your products on one of the biggest websites in the world with no fees. You will potentially reach a whole new audience, you'll have the opportunity to have front-of-mind marketing with these people, as well as new traffic to your website and/or foot traffic to your actual store.

The impact of a strong cover photo

When I talk about cover photos, I'm talking about the cover photo areas you have available on platforms like Twitter, Facebook Business Pages and LinkedIn. They are the rectangle photos that appear at the top of your profiles and are placed behind your bio photo.

First, how do you create a cover photo for platforms such as the ones mentioned above? My top suggestion is to head to www.canva.com. Canva is an online design platform that offers user-friendly tools and templates to create a wide range of graphics, from presentations and social media posts to logos and print materials – basically it's a non-designers heaven. You can find a Canva template that is the right size, to make it easier for yourself. There might even be a template you love you can use and that would make even easier – I am all for easy.

Second, the golden rule is "a picture paints a thousand words," so what do you want your cover photo to say about you, your business, what's going on in your business? For example, if you're a speaker, then a photo of you speaking to an audience says what you do via a photo. If you sell candles, you'd feature candles – you get the point. Make sure your cover photo also has a call-to-action in it – a call to the person viewing it to take another step into your world. Calls to action will vary depending on your business and what season of business you are in but could be as simple as "visit my website" with a link or "download 108 Social Media Content Creation Ideas" or "get a bonus belt when you buy one of our new season dresses". Don't leave one of the best pieces of real estate on your social media accounts, your cover photos, without a call to action – it's a waste, and you need to be more strategic in business.

Third, how often should you change a cover photo? I would say seasonally. I am not necessarily talking about winter, spring, summer, autumn seasons, although you can use them. What other seasons do you have in your business? Christmas, Easter, Father's Day, End of the Financial Year, new product launch, NAIDOC Week – there's tonnes of them. Think of the ones that your business would like more promotion for and use your cover photo to express them. If you don't embrace this method of changing for the seasons of your business, at least change them three or four times a year to keep them up to date.

Have a memorable bio photo

Now you might not think that your bio photo is part of your marketing strategy, but it is. Showing up for your audience, letting them get to know you is a crucial part of your marketing strategy and your bio picture does play a part in that.

So, some preliminary questions – is your bio picture, on any of your social media platforms, you? Recent you? If not, then make it you today. I often get asked if the bio photo should be your business logo – the answer is almost always no, it should be you. Your logo means something to you, but not really much to anyone else. Most people who are following you, interacting with you, looking to buy from you, would like to know two things – who you are, aka what you look like, and your name. If it's not easy to know these two pieces of information by looking at your social media, then you are one thousand percent leaving money on the table.

If we head back to the years prior to social media, every one of your customers would have known what you looked like and probably your name because the only ways they would have interacted with you was in person – in your shop, store, office or at a market. We need to stop hiding behind our products and services and bring you to the forefront of your business for your customers, who spend their hard-earned money with you, to get to know you. Don't you owe them at least that?

I had a face-to-face marketing session with a lady I only knew from social media a few years ago. She lived locally to me, so I agreed to meet in person. She arrived at the café and sat down, said hello and started chatting. I had no idea who this person was. She knew me as my picture is everywhere online, but her bio picture was at least 20 years old, because she looked nothing like what I was expecting. It took me a while to adjust and realise this was my client, the one I was expecting, but she looked so different.

You are just you – so show up online as you.

> **You are just you – so show up online as you.**

If you have a large team, the answer to the bio picture might be different. But if you are the person selling – answering the emails, answering the phones, answering the questions, posting on social media and the person behind the business – then start showing up. Making your bio photo a recent picture of you is the quickest way to start building trust.

PS – make sure your name is somewhere to be seen, too! It doesn't matter whether you sign off your social media posts with your name or your name is evident in the bio or the page name – just make sure it is there.

CHALLENGE

So, you know the challenge for this chapter – update your bio picture and put your name all over your socials and in your bios.

Leveraging Facebook Groups for business

Facebook Groups are one of those marketing strategies that small businesses don't give enough time to. We are so busy posting on our own pages and profiles, and ticking the "I've done my marketing" box, we forget what social media is really all about. Being social.

Finding Facebook Groups where your ideal customer and your community is hanging out and getting involved in those groups is the best way to use Facebook these days. Now, you can't go into groups and always post "buy my stuff". We have to go back to what social media is all about – being social – so therefore we have to be social in groups as well. Being social as a business owner is all about giving value to others in the community.

Can you sell in other people's Facebook Groups? Yes, absolutely – but there are two things to be aware of:

1. What sort of group it is – is the whole idea of the group to let people post about their business or not?

2. Be really respectful of the admins who have created the group and monitor it every day to make it a safe space for you to come and be social on social media.

My experience with Facebook Groups is vast. I have one that is my business group where I invite my community to come and hang out, be social, learn and promote themselves – it's called Like Minded Business Owners – if you're not a member, come join!

My other major group is one I created in October 2019 when there were horrific droughts down mainly the eastern states of Australia. It's called Buy From a Bush Business and was created to help small rural businesses get more sales coming into Christmas 2020. That group currently has over 370,000 members. (I don't manage the admin for that group anymore, as I have a team who helps out because it is so big.) This group, in particular, has changed the lives of many rural and regional business owners and injected more than 10 million dollars back into the rural and regional economy. I am pretty proud of what I created there – maybe you're a member? I have loads of other groups I manage, including a few local groups but the above two are my main groups.

Not all Facebook Groups allow you to join as your business name – but some do. It's up to the admin who set up the group whether that's a feature allowed or not. As mentioned before, be really respectful of the person who created and manages the admin for any groups you are in or join. It's a big job and some members make it hard by not following the rules. What are the rules? Each Facebook Group does have rules. They are generally pinned to the side of your screen if you are looking on a PC or laptop or you can find them under the About section if on your phone. Read them and follow them. Take note of when you can promote under the rules – some groups have promotional days when you can post about your business. Do not go in there and start selling or posting about your business without reading the rules. That is just rude. Not respecting the rules put in place by the admin, in the words of The 12th Man – "it's just not cricket".

I have a spreadsheet pinned above my desk with the Facebook Groups I am in (or the ones I want to be involved with the most) and the days available for posting. I refer to that each week and post accordingly.

I'd recommend you spend 10-15 minutes a week hanging out and posting in different Facebook Groups, always with your business goals in mind.

> **CHALLENGE**
> That is your homework for this chapter. Join the groups where your community hangs out, read the rules, make notes of any days you are allowed to post what or sell and have it handy to refer to each week.

> **BONUS TIP**
> Facebook Groups are a great place to find opportunities for your business. There might be TV, newspapers, magazines, blogs looking for articles, stories or blog posts you can submit, as well as podcasters looking for guests.

Using LinkedIn groups to grow

There are probably only two comments for this marketing strategy:

1. Read Facebook groups above and follow my thoughts, ideas and rules there.
2. LinkedIn groups, at the time of reading this, are not worth it. Don't bother. Move onto another strategy that is worth your time. LinkedIn even makes it hard to find groups, so clearly, they aren't interested in building them for us either.

You need a reach out strategy

If you feel that you are posting on social media and not getting a return on that investment of time and energy, then this is possibly where you are going wrong – you don't have a reach out strategy. A reach out strategy is just that – reaching out to others strategically.

Reach out strategies

- Spend time on social media being social (as you and your business).
- Spend time on social media especially 15 before and 15 minutes after posting so the algorithm gives you more love. It works, it really does but unfortunately, none of us have 30 minutes to

dedicate to each post we do. But it's worth thinking about and remembering that this is how things work in the world of social media algorithms. I am not advocating you do it, just letting you know this is how it works.

- Spend time commenting back to people who comment on your posts – ask them something – encourage more engagement. This is vitally important. If you walked into a party and someone said "hello" to you, you wouldn't walk past them without replying – would you? So, don't do it on social media either. If someone spends their time engaging with you, you owe them the same courtesy.
- Post into Facebook Groups with your ideal client in them – see the earlier tip for Facebook Groups for ideas and suggestions.
- Lead with value – add value first – build know, like and trust. Think give, give, give, then ask.
- Spend time commenting strategically on other people's posts (giving value/answering questions).

A good marketing strategy has the following two parts:

1. It markets your business to the right people at the right time in the right places to help you reach your goals.
2. It has a reach out strategy, especially on social media – after all, it is called social media for a reason. It's not called *one-way communication buy my stuff* media. We have to be social on social media but as business owners we need to be strategic about it and spend our marketing time wisely.

If you feel like social media is a waste of time and you aren't getting anything back from it, I would humbly suggest that this is the reason why – there's no social in your social media.

CHALLENGE
Challenge yourself to set aside 10–15 minutes, twice a week, to go to your Facebook Page's feed and start commenting, liking and sharing posts from the people your page follows. Similarly, do the same on your Instagram feed (and any other platforms you are on). Think of it as a your Hansel and Gretel strategy – sprinkling your brand breadcrumbs everywhere.

"

If you feel like social media is a waste of time and you aren't getting anything back from it, I would humbly suggest that this is the reason why – there's no social in your social media.

"

The dynamics of social media takeovers

What's a social media takeover? It's when you log in as someone else on social media, with their permission, of course, and/or that person logs in as you and literally takes over your social media for, potentially, that day. They post in your stories about their day, their offers, their business.

Side note: A social media takeover is normally done in stories – not in a person's feed.

Why would you do this or allow this? Simple – to get in front of someone else's audience that looks like yours but potentially isn't yours. And vice versa. This works really well as a marketing strategy if it is done like a collaboration – so equal use of each other's social media. Of course, you need to put some rules in place so your audience knows what is going on and doesn't think you've been hacked. For example:

- How long does the takeover last for?
- How do you promote it beforehand?
- What outcome are both of you are expecting from this marketing strategy?
- Can you add links to your content for their audience to go to?
- Are you allowed to sell your products/services?

As long as everyone is aware before you do the takeover, it could be a great collaboration between business colleagues or friends.

If you've never tried a social media takeover before, choose a business friend, have a chat and see if they are keen. Of course, be strategic and make sure that your audiences are similar – you don't want to damage each other's audiences by providing them with content they are in no way interested in. For example, if their social media is always about eating healthily and you sell fairy floss, it might not be a good collaboration for either audience!

Understanding the pros and cons of the blue tick

The Blue Tick or Meta Verified is something we can now pay to get on our Instagram and Facebook profile. This is Meta's next iteration on making some more coin from us and really bringing the platform from free to paid for small business owners, regardless of whether you do paid marketing. I am not a fan, as you will read below.

So, what does the blue tick mean? It's basically a way of verifying the authenticity of your account. It says to the world "this account is real, this account owner is genuine". It can quickly build trust and credibility with your followers.

A verified account is "more likely" to be seen by a wider audience, but that's yet to be proven. Certainly, the unpaid version of the blue tick did this, but the paid model is yet to prove itself.

Side note: You have been able to apply for the blue tick for many years, but now you pay for it.

I have two problems with this. First, and this one is my cranky one: just because Meta couldn't work out a way to stop our accounts being hacked, IDs stolen and being scammed by fake accounts, now we have to pay to be authentic? I think it's a cop-out. And a little of "how dare you". You created the platform, you allowed bots and baddies to get an account, but now it's up to us to ensure our own safety and pay for that safety … This is such a big business thing to do – make the little people pay for a problem they created.

Second, will it work – is it worth it? My answer – maybe. As with most new features on platforms like this, if you are an early adopter, you might see some extra reach. But as it becomes mainstream and everyone who's authentic has a blue tick, then I can't see how it will help get you more reach, because everyone can't get more reach, right? And what happens if you don't have a blue tick and everyone else does – will your authenticity be questioned?

Of course, it's not all about reach, they say you'll also get access to new features, improved security, priority support (like there's any non-priority support) and more opportunities to collaborate – whatever that means.

If you want to know more, look it up here: https://about.meta.com/technologies/meta-verified.

Whether you should get the blue tick and be verified or not is a wait and see game. At the time of writing this book, I am still playing the waiting game, interested in others' feedback. But if you head to my socials and I do have the blue tick by the time you read this, know that I have done so to test, measure and report back – after all, that is my job as a marketing thought leader! So, watch this space.

Design an effective DM strategy

Social media is all about being social – it's in the name. Therefore, it makes total sense to have a good DM strategy. What's a DM strategy? Or what's a DM? Let's start there.

DM is shorthand for "direct message," sometimes we also use PM which stands for "private message." They are same same. A DM is a private message sent on social media platforms. It's a personalised way to communicate directly with customers and followers.

Why would you create a DM strategy for your business? First, because it is a great way to build community. It adds a personal touch to your marketing and allows you to communicate one-on-one with a follower or a connection. They can ask you questions, you can answer them (promptly, of course) and it can also be used to make more sales.

E-commerce does this really well – selling through DMs. You can send exclusive offers to certain customers, reward loyal followers, share products or service suggestions with them and really personalise their shopping experience with you.

Of course, as with all communication with prospects and customers, it's important not to spam them by sending too many DMs. It's important to be genuine, respectful and to listen to their needs or concerns before offering solutions – because otherwise that's just spamming.

If you have a DM strategy, avoid generic messages (the same message to everyone). This strategy is about building community and connecting, not spamming. On LinkedIn, I send a personalised voice DM to everyone (or 99%) of the people who reach out and want to connect with me. It's a really nice way to introduce yourself and for me, it's a great way to stand out in a crowded marketplace because hardly anyone else takes the time to send a voice connection message. I try to do the same on Instagram, but I have to say I am less efficient on that platform for some darn reason – but I do try and send connection messages to new connections on that platform, too.

These are just two examples of how you could use a DM strategy to build your community. But how do you start the conversations – how do you get them into your DMs in the first place? Well, other than new connections and sending them a message, you strategically ask people to DM you through your social media posts. For example, if you post a wonderful social media post with a great piece of education for your community, you can say, "If you want more information, DM me". Or if polls are part of your engagement strategy, you can ask, "Do you prefer to read blogs or listen to podcasts?" To everyone who answered, "read blogs", you send them a DM asking them whose blogs they read because you'd love to add some more great blogs to your reading list or share with your audience. Perhaps you could suggest one of your own with a link, and to everyone who responded to podcasts, you could do something similar. Or use Instagram story stickers to create polls or interaction, and again, DM people who responded with a simple DM message.

DMs are just about creating deeper conversations on the platform but away from the public. They are about standing out from the crowded marketplace and about building community and connections.

Investing smartly in paid social media ads

Not all marketing is free and not all marketing should be free. It is important that we invest in our marketing, and as the old saying goes, "We have to spend money to make money". Every small business should have a marketing budget. Historically, a marketing budget has been around 2-5% of your annual turnover (not profit), and realistically more than that for new and unestablished businesses.

One way of spending your marketing budget is on digital ads, such as Facebook, Instagram, LinkedIn, X (formally known as Twitter) and/or Pinterest pins. Of course, there's also Google ads and Google Shopping ads but more on them in Tip #102.

Ideas for social media ads

- **Assume nothing, test everything.** If you are wondering whether this image will work better than that image, there's no way to tell but to test. So, when you are getting your ad creatives together with copy, photos and videos, it's best practice to set up two to four ads with different creatives and/or different audiences. This is the only way you'll be able to work out what works.

- **Start with the end in mind.** Start with the end desired result and work backwards. If I wanted to have my new eBook Ultimate Guide to Facebook Ads downloaded 100 times each month, and I know that 50% of people who land on my landing page sign up, then I need 200 leads to go to my landing page for a conversion rate of 50%.

  If I average, on a traffic objective ad, $1.50 per click, and I need 200 people clicking to get 100 downloads, then my budget has to be at least $300. I also know that 10% of people who see my ad, click. So, I need 2000 people to see my ad.

  That's what start with the end in mind looks like.

- **Great offers sell without selling.** If you have a good offer in place, you have more chances to create an ad that pays off. That's a fact. They sell without selling and remember, people don't like being sold to, but they love to buy stuff.

  Set aside some time to tinker around, start a few test campaigns, and see what happens. Like anything, it takes practice to get good at it.

My advice: get started now. When's the best time to plant a tree? Twenty years ago. When's the next best time – TODAY.

There are four mistakes I see online marketers (that's you – if you're on social media, you're an online marketer) make constantly with their ads.

1. Frankly, the first one I see people make offline as well. And it's just so important. There's no goal for the advert. They haven't set a goal of "I want to build my database by 400 people" or "I want to increase my profits for this month by 10%" or sell 320 courses or 12 pallets of stock. There's no metric of success. No way to tell, when the ad ends, if it worked or not.

2. You are putting the wrong message to the wrong audience at the wrong time. Lots of Facebook ads experts talk about targeting. Make sure you know who you are targeting and that you know your ideal client avatar and who your who is. Trust me, it's crucially important but point three below is even more important.

3. Something not enough Facebook ads experts talk about is where your ideal client sits when it comes to their buyer journey with you.

   You may know your avatar, the people you'd like to attract more of in your business because you know if you get more of them, then your business will soar. But those avatars sit in three different audience types:

   a. **Cold traffic:** These are the people who have never heard of you or your brand. They have had no interactions or dealings with you at all.
   b. **Warm traffic:** These people at least know who you are. They may have liked your Facebook business page or followed you on Instagram. They have some idea of who you are and what you offer.
   c. **Hot traffic:** These people are your fans! They engage with you on social media, they are on your email list, and they have already purchased something from you.

   So even though you know your avatar, you need to make sure you are serving up the right ad with the right call to action to them where they are in the buyer's journey – from learning who you are to buying from you.

   There's no use serving an ad to completely cold traffic saying, "Click here to buy my $1000 program." They have literally no idea who you are or what you do or if you can serve them.

To a completely cold audience you might be better off serving them a video ad with some amazing information-based value to get them to watch it. Then perhaps retarget them with a follow-up ad with a different call to action, because now they at least know who you are and a little of what you do and your expertise.

4. They never go back and check to see if the ad is actually working or not. No matter how long you set up an ad for, make sure you go back in and check around 48-72 hours later, to see how the ad is tracking. If you set up an ad but don't check if it reaches the goal you set for it, you have wasted your time, energy and money.

   When you place an ad on Facebook, Google, Instagram or LinkedIn, please oh please, go back about 48-72 hours later (depending on the platform and targeting required) and check it. Make sure it's hitting the goals you set for it, make sure it's working and if not, switch it off altogether or edit it and set it going again.

Social media paid marketing is not a set and forget strategy.

The secret to successful digital ads is understanding that the algorithm (on any platform) will do exactly what you tell it to do. It'll find the exact people you asked for and get them to do the exact call to action you've asked for, too.

I'll give you an example. Traffic. Traffic is the objective you would choose to drive people from Facebook to any URL you choose, such as your website's landing page, a blog post or app.

So, Facebook will find the people, according to your targeting, who are the people most likely to click an ad with the objective of driving them off Facebook to wherever you've sent them – blog, website, landing page or sales page.

But that's it. That's the secret – that is all it will do and that's all it will guarantee.

So, if you just thought, "Yay, that's awesome – it will give me traffic to my website to buy my product", then you'd be wrong – very wrong.

Now, disclaimer, I'm not saying you won't get sales from this objective, but what I am saying is that Facebook is not necessarily sending traffic who are most likely to BUY to your sales page – they are only sending traffic who are most likely to CLICK the ad and go to the page.

"

Social media paid marketing is not a set and forget strategy.

"

If you want people who are most likely to buy, if you want Facebook to send people who are most likely to BUY, then you'll need to use the conversions objective. Because that objective is set up to convert people – just like it says.

So, whenever you are spending money on digital ads, think about what you want (the goal) and work backwards from there, remembering the ad will do exactly what you tell it, no more, no less, so be hyper aware of what you are asking it to do.

> **BONUS TIP**
> If you want to do some paid marketing on platforms such as Facebook, head to YouTube and watch some videos and learn from people who are experts in that field. Start by searching for Facebook ads for beginners.

Understanding the potential of Pinterest

Now if you're thinking "Jenn, Pinterest isn't actually a social media platform, it's a search engine", then you'd be completely correct. But, you see, I don't have a search engine part of the book, so I am sneaking it in here under social media. Pinterest is a great way to market your business.

Pinterest can be a valuable tool for your business's marketing strategy but you do need to think of it more like posting on to Google than posting on to Facebook. It's more like putting something on a search engine as opposed to a social media site. Because they do act differently.

Pinterest has about six million monthly active users in Australia. Of course, in the US, that stat is more like 99 million. The platform has more female than male users as well.

What I love about Pinterest is that content doesn't get old. If someone is searching for content that has your keywords in it (keywords are key with Pinterest, along with great visuals), just like Google, it doesn't matter if that content is five years old or five minutes old. It's all about its searchability rather than its chronological order. Therefore, Pinterest is a longer strategy than posting on socials. Pinterest can continue to drive traffic and engagement over long periods of time.

Pinterest is all about the visual and therefore serves as an inspirational hub for searchable content. The most popular content on the platform is craft, fashion, food, weddings and home renovations. I have a Pinterest account (come find me – https://www.pinterest.com.au/socialwithjenn) and I spend money hiring a Pinterest expert a few times a year updating my content. I have to admit, being someone who sells services rather than products, Pinterest does not get into my Top Three lead-generating platforms, according to my Google Analytics. So, I pin and post, and get around 225,000 views a month to my content, but it doesn't necessarily lead to leads and sales.

You can run Pinterest ads, which are called "promoted pins" but we aren't going to go into those in this chapter. Basically, promoted pins are all about showcasing your products, driving traffic to your website and increasing engagement with your content.

BONUS TIP

Even if you aren't on Pinterest for your business, get on there for inspiration for your own content. There is so much content over there to get inspired by and any search results are so different to that of a search engine like Google.

Navigating the new Threads by Meta

Threads is the latest addition to the social media landscape and at the time of writing this book, it is pretty new and about 100 million of us are on the platform, working out how to use it.

Threads is Meta's Twitter. Threads is about community and I have to say, right now, I am here for it. I love that we are all new, all trying to work out what to post, when to post, what works, what is not working and all the good juicy bits that marketers like me adore.

Using Threads for business

If you are one of the 100 million accounts already on Threads and wondering how to use it for business, here are some simple hints:

- This social media platform, right now, is all about connection and community. Think about creating and repurposing content that is community orientated and will create community.

- Be you – this is your opportunity to just be you. Don't try and be anyone else. Authentic is an overused word, but showing up on Threads just as you are is perfect.

- Click yes to "connect with people you are already connected with on Instagram" as you go through the process of signing up. Imagine having another space, a new space, to nurture those who have already had an interaction with you on another platform. Warm audiences are so much better than cold.

- Do the usual stuff you do on other platforms – share content that's educational, entertaining, inspiring and yes, make some sales by sharing how people can buy from you.

- Finally and importantly, engage, engage, engage. Engage with others – have a darn good reach out strategy and spend time being social in your brand-new community of only 100 million members (yikes!).

The art of repurposing content

I am sure you will agree that there's a lot of time, effort and energy that goes into creating consistent original content for your marketing. A LOT OF WORK. So, it doesn't really make sense to do it, share it once or twice and move on to the next one but it's a pattern I see consistently with content creators. (PS: That's you, you are a content creator because you are in business.)

Despite what some believe, not everyone sees everything you put on social media or opens every piece of email marketing you send. Therefore, putting it under their nose more than once is necessary to build traction, build movement and build your expertise. If they don't see it or read it or watch it, they won't know how brilliant you are.

Ideas for repurposing content

See the list below of some simple ways you can repurpose content, getting more mileage out of the hard work you put into creating a piece of marketing content. You could:

- turn a blog post into a video or podcast episode
- submit your blog to a media outlet for free PR
- use customer reviews as social media posts or testimonials on your website
- create a slide deck from a white paper or report
- turn a list into an infographic
- take social media feed posts and turn them into stories or reels
- take longer form social media posts or blogs and turn them into a LinkedIn article
- use statistics or quotes from a report in social media graphics or ads
- use images from your content to create social media posts or Pinterest pins
- create a webinar or live stream from a how-to guide or tutorial
- turn a series of related social media posts into a blog post or article
- use the content of a successful social media post as the basis for an email or newsletter
- create an ebook or guide from a series of social media posts on a specific topic
- turn a live video or Q&A session into a blog post or podcast episode
- use a successful social media post to create a testimonial or case study for your website
- create a presentation or slide deck from a series of related social media posts
- use a series of social media posts to create a mini course or online workshop
- use a successful social media post to create an advertisement for your product or service

> **The number one reason you should be on social media is to get people OFF social media and onto your email list.**

- turn a collection of social media posts into a visual portfolio to showcase your work
- use a successful social media post as the basis for a press release or media pitch
- create an email series from a longer piece of content
- share social media content into Facebook groups or Instagram private group posts
- turn video content into a YouTube Channel.

Repurposing content is all about making the most of what you've already created and the possibilities for repurposing social media and other marketing content are endless. Don't be afraid to get creative and think outside the box to make the most of your marketing efforts. Repurposing content is a great way to reach new audiences, reinforce your message, and get more value out of the content you've already created. So, get creative and see how many different ways you can share your message with the world.

> **BONUS TIP**
>
> If you're short on time for your marketing, repurposing is your piece of marketing gold.

Social media is a necessary evil in business right now. You simply need to be on the platforms, the right platforms, to market to your customers and potential customers. But, here's the kicker.

The number one reason you should be on social media is to get people OFF social media and onto your email list.

Social media is a great place to meet new people, attract new prospects, but your email list is the best place to nurture them until they are ready to buy or buy again. See Chapter 7 about email marketing a bit later in the book.

Book Bonus: If you head to the back of the book you will find a QR code, scan that QR code and choose 365 days of Social Media Tips and get my free book of one year of social media content tips. Now that should help make marketing simple!

***

Social media is such a big subject. I hope the tips above gave you some clarity about the marketing you are already doing and stretched your thinking to push you to do either more of what's working for you, or to try something a little different.

If a small business owner comes to me and says, "Jenn, I don't have time for marketing but know I need to do some. What do you suggest I do?", my answer is always, video. Live video. You can literally pick up your phone, click live, talk for two to three minutes, upload to the platform. Boom – your marketing for that day is done! So, if you are time poor, do more video.

Make marketing a priority. Use social media to grow your community, but I'd love to encourage you to keep reading and thinking outside the "social media square" and do more marketing than just social media marketing. Your profits will thank you later.

Chapter 3
TIMELESS TACTICS
Reimagining classic marketing

When our business community is successful, our broader community is successful.

——

Mell Millgate, Starfish Marketing, Rutherglen, Victoria

Do the classic ways of marketing still work in a digital, tech world? 100%. Absolutely. In fact, some of them will work BETTER than they used to. For instance, let's take the simple act of sending out an invitation to an event – using snail mail (aka mail).

Let's say that the envelope is bright pink and addressed in handwriting – do you think the targeted person will be so curious that they won't be able to resist opening the letter to see what's in it? Of course not. Who gets bright pink, handwritten envelopes anymore? You are guaranteed, as long as they are addressed correctly, a 100% open rate of that envelope. Now you can't get a 100% open rate on any email, can you?

So, yes classic marketing strategies do still work. Below, I'll explain how to use them in our tech driven, digital age of business. But there's two questions you must ask yourself before applying any marketing strategy, including the classic ones, otherwise, they won't work.

- Question 1 – Who is your who?
- Question 2 – Where do they hang out?

If you are running a TV advert to your ideal client who rarely watches TV because they always watch streaming services – then TV won't work.

If you've invested in your local newspaper for an advert to market your new range of winter jumpers which your female customers (mostly aged over 65) love, then there's a chance your investment into print media will work. Only, of course, if you know your female customers, aged 65-plus, actually read the newspaper.

So, as you can see, it's not the marketing strategy and whether it still works or not, it's simply the question of does it work for YOUR audience.

Classic or digital marketing – it really doesn't matter. Both work – they simply work on different targeted audiences.

Budget often comes into it, too – as to whether it will be a successful campaign or not. Obviously, to run a TV campaign is thousands, sometimes tens of thousands of dollars, so running a TV campaign is often out of our reach as small business owners. That's why we don't do it, rather than the fact that it doesn't work.

Marketing is all about touchpoints. How many times your ideal audience sees your marketing. How many times they interact with your marketing. Unless you have the marketing budget of say the "golden arches" (Maccas), then a one-off marketing campaign using just one marketing strategy is unlikely to yield the return on investment that you need. Maccas ads on TV work to make us take action and remember what they are promoting this month because we also see it on our socials, in our newspapers, on websites that we land on because they are paying for that space too. It's about touchpoints, not one, not two, but seemingly, sometimes, being everywhere.

So, my advice is if you are going to invest large amounts of money into your marketing, spread the dollars and spread the message across many different platforms and strategies – potentially classic and new. Offline and online.

So, let's dive in now – let's have a look at some of the classic marketing strategies that still work.

Get your brand on television

Running a TV ad campaign can be extremely expensive and is out of the budget of most small business owners. If you're considering making that investment of running a TV advert, then you really need to know your customer. You need to know that they will not only be watching TV, but watching at that time of the day or night, and that they are the sort of people who watch ads, as opposed to switching channels between shows and that they have the budget to buy what it is that you are selling.

Sounds tough, yes? For sure – it's not easy. And the creative directors at the TV station you are considering working with will also have an impact on whether your advert is a success or not. So, you really need to have a good idea of what you want your ad to say, and what your call to action is going to be for the consumer who watches it.

How do you know what you want your ad to look like, sound like and make your consumer feel after they have watched it? Well, my book writing coach told me if I wanted to write a remarkable book, I had to read more books. So if you want to run an engaging, profitable TV campaign, then start watching ads and seeing what you like and what you don't like. Do the research.

Recently, there's been some adverts on TV that have used QR codes really well. The advert is not very creative, but the call to action is strong (scan the code) and the strategy of getting them from the TV to taking action after they have seen the ad is, I would imagine, strong. Or at least stronger than passively watching, as is the case with 99% of other ads.

If you want to know how to do TV ad campaigns (or really any marketing campaign to be honest) well, then watch infomercials. I love infomercials. The precise marketing tactics they use to get you to buy is truly magical (and not always in a good way). But, even as a seasoned marketer who teaches this stuff to other small business owners, I still want to buy the mop. I know it's crap and it's not going to do everything they tell me it will, but their marketing is just so good, I want to buy it too.

Love or hate infomercials, I would encourage you to take some time and watch one or two. Watch them with your marketing hat on as a business owner, not as the consumer who wants to buy. Take note of the formula they use, the language they use and the calls to action they consistently use as well. It is super interesting.

The title of this chapter is Get your brand on television – and you don't always have to pay for that.

To get your brand on TV, think outside the square a little. Later in the book, I will talk about Public Relations (PR) as a marketing strategy – see Tip #86 – but getting on TV by going down the PR strategy is a great way to get some free airtime on television.

I've been on TV loads of times for free. I've been interviewed on Channel 10, Sky News, and on morning shows, all for free. How? Well, I will leave the bulk of how to my tip on PR, but basically it was because I had something interesting for their audience to hear about. It wasn't about making the sale, it wasn't part of my sales strategy, it was part of my brand awareness strategy (remember we talked about the five different strategies in Tip #6).

So TV can be done for free or you can pay for a campaign. Your desired outcome – sales or brand awareness – is how you will measure the success of the campaign.

Using radio to market your business

Does radio still work? Yep. Country radio, local radio, community radio – they all work a little differently to our "big smoke" stations and the price to advertise on them reflects these differences.

You are going to get pretty sick of my saying this, if you read this book cover to cover, but it is fundamentally the most important information I can teach you. To know if radio is going to work for you, you need to know if your audience, your buyer, your ideal client or customer actually listens to radio.

There are some bloody terrific radio ads though. Their brand awareness is amazing and I am sure their brand awareness turns into profit, otherwise, they'd stop doing it, right?

If I said, "Frank Walker from National Tiles" to you – would you be able to precisely hear the voice of Frank and recall the ad? It's a radio ad that's burned into my brain – I hate it, his voice drives me insane but that's not the point. The point of the ad is to make me think, "I need new tiles for my house, I'll go to National Tiles." Because that's the brand I associate with tiles for my house because of that stupid ad.

Another radio advert that I love is local to me, so you probably haven't heard it. A local tyre company in Albury, NSW, runs a radio ad campaign (and TV too) to sell more tyres – not so interesting, right? Wrong. The strategy he uses in this ad is so creative that it made it into my book.

He doesn't talk about his tyres on the ad but that's what he wants to sell you. He talks about all the businesses he sells tyres to that you might know, and the line is "we got them there". The local plumber – "we got them there [to you]". The local RACV van – "we got them there". The local morning tea mobile van – "we got them there."

This ad is genius in so many ways. Firstly, he's standing out from all his competitors who also sell tyres with an ad that's not actually trying to sell you tyres – he's actually selling without selling. He's positioning himself as a community man, as he's effectively using his air-time to also market other businesses. (I don't know if the businesses he talks about contribute financially – I am assuming they don't). He's making selling tyres, something all rural people need, almost a community service. And there's nothing about money – no prices. He is not entering the marketplace of tyre selling as the cheapest or with a deal – it's all about helping the people you need in your life to get to you there safely.

And finally, if your business was mentioned in this advert, you would share with your customers, yes? Absolutely. So, he's creating viral content for micro-influencers (the businesses he's mentioned) and connecting into new audiences all the time by giving shout-outs to other business owners who might have customers who don't use them for their tyres ... Yet.

It's genius. I cannot tell you how much I love this campaign. Does it work, does it bring him new customers and more profit and a good return on investment? I can't see how it wouldn't.

The possibilities of you doing something similar are endless, even if it's not on radio. Simply tagging businesses on Facebook that you help could have the same desired effect. Think outside the marketing box.

You should always end a radio ad with your business name. I have often caught the end of an ad and thought – which business was that? Think about how we were taught to answer a phone professionally – "Welcome to the Kitchenware Queens, this is Jenn." The customer remembers Jenn, the last word – that's all I need them to remember, as they knew who they were calling. Compare this to – "Welcome to the Kitchenware Queens, Jenn speaking." They remember "speaking", not Jenn. Same with radio – end with your business name every, single, time.

Before I finish up with radio, just like with television, you can get radio for free too using a PR strategy.

Like many marketing strategies, radio marketing should not be done in isolation but if done at all, should be done as part of a whole campaign and is simply one touchpoint in a series of many for the customer you are targeting. And, it goes without saying, we need to ensure our customers/client or prospects are radio listeners for this to work.

Weighing the value of local newspaper ads

Do local newspaper ads still work? My answer to this is not any different to the last two types of media, television and radio. Yes, it still works, but only if your ideal client or customer, your buyer, actually reads the newspaper.

There is no doubt that newspapers, especially in country areas, are struggling to keep up with the digital age and many are stuck in the era of 20 years ago and simply not moving forward.

My amazing retail friend Michelle, who has Judds in Yarrawonga, still puts ads in the local paper and still puts a printed catalogue inside the newspaper a few times a year and it works. Why? Because the clothing she is marketing is 100% directed towards the demographic that buys the newspaper and reads it. She doesn't try marketing her surfy brands in the newspaper, just the clothing ranges she knows works for her.

Do you still read newspapers? I have to say that I am a page flicker and a picture looker. I don't read it cover to cover, I do look at the pictures, and the "hatched, matched and dispatched" section – births, deaths and marriages. My parents send the newspaper out to me – I pay for it but they get it because my local newsagent won't deliver to the farm. Australia Post couldn't possibly add a newspaper to their delivery, like they used to – my in-laws used to have bread and milk delivered to the farm by the postie – but I digress.

So, if you want to see if newspaper advertising is for you, you could also try some adverts in the classifieds – where lots of eyeballs go rather than in the general part of the paper where things could be missed.

When I had a local retail business, the Kitchenware Queens, we had a spot each week in the local newspaper where we supplied them with a recipe. Same placement every week, so people knew where to find the recipe. It was good branding and had a strong call to action, and it worked.

But we also used that recipe in our weekly e-newsletter, printed it to place on our counter for people to take away with them, used it on our social media and had it placed strategically in the window of our shop under the heading "recipe of the week".

Advertising in the newspaper worked, in that it kept us top of mind, had good brand awareness around it but it was just one touchpoint in our whole marketing strategy. That, in my opinion, is why it worked.

Of course, as with television and radio, you can get some print-time in your local newspaper for free with a PR strategy. You could write an opinion piece, an informational piece, and value-adding piece for them to print at no cost to you. Newspaper advertising is just another touchpoint in your overall marketing strategy, it's NOT your whole marketing strategy.

The timeless charm of business cards

With the world of business being more and more environmentally conscious of its carbon footprint, you will often hear people say they are doing away with the humble, printed, business card.

So, this presents you with two amazing opportunities.

First, be innovative with your business card by taking it digital and surprising and delighting your contact. If LinkedIn or Instagram are your thing, they can create a unique QR code you simply bring up on your phone and the other person taps – you are now connected.

The second amazing opportunity is to stand out by having a tangible business card. If no-one at an event or networking opportunity has one, then people taking yours home in their pocket presents an opportunity like no other to stand out.

You can still be environmentally friendly with your card. You can use recycled paper or you can donate money to an environmental cause each time you do a print run (put this on your card so people know). You can have it infused with seeds for the garden, so once your potential customers have finished with your card, they can plant it and have a special treat from it for long after your business transaction is done. Imagine someone using your chives in their cooking long after you've exchanged business cards. As long as they are good gardeners and water their plants, that is – me, not so much.

There is something physiological about handing someone your business card, having that moment of eye contact and possible touch contact that sets you apart from anyone else.

If you are going to print business cards – be innovative. I have my photo on mine so if I am at an event with hundreds of people and people are taking home a pocket of business cards, they won't forget Jenn. Because my picture is staring back at them from the card, I am no longer the face they can't remember – I am the face they do remember.

You can put your business card in a cello bag with a mint or a chocky to be memorable. You could put a QR code on your card so when they scan it they get something of value for free – surprise and delight. That something could be a freebie check list or a downloadable document to help them do something specific. Or even a voucher for a free coffee at their local coffee shop – although that might be hard to do in the country with not many franchise coffee shops around. Of course, the beauty of the QR code is you can change where it takes them after scanning, so you could potentially tailor it for every event. Interesting thought, yes?

I'm pro business card. But if you're not with me, then be innovative with your connection approach, your data giving and data collecting approach and don't let the opportunities of connecting with others pass you by.

Your net worth is very relevant to your network.

Advertising on the move with your car

This is certainly a marketing strategy from years gone by – it's as old as cars possibly.

But do you know what my number one hate with cars or vehicles that have their name on them? Transport companies, not all but some, are the worst at this. Dirty vehicles. You have your name all over your vehicle and it's filthy dirty. Not "I've been down a dirt road recently" dirt, but grime and mud that has clearly been there for a length of time.

Remember, way back in this book, I spoke about marketing being everything and how everything you say and do says something about you whether you meant it to or not? Well, a filthy, dirty vehicle says to me that you don't care about your business and if you don't care about your business, then you probably don't care too much about your customers or clients. Or if it's a staff member's vehicle, they don't take much care or pride.

" Your net worth is very relevant to your network. **"**

So, if you have your name on your vehicle, or are thinking about it, remember what it's saying about you.

Another pet hate with signage on a vehicle is the symbols for Facebook and Instagram. Who really cares? All your competition is on there too. At least tell me your handle so I can find you, not just that you are on there – somewhere. Use a QR code to take them to a "link tree" – that way they can choose their own adventure.

A link tree is a page on your website that the QR code is connected to. Once it's scanned, it takes them to that page which has options to click, for instance, your Facebook page, Instagram account, website, LinkedIn, latest freebie, a map of where your business is. The possibilities are endless and the best thing, with a web page like this, is you can add more options or retire others as you go.

So, I haven't answered the question of whether you should put your business name on your car or vehicle. The answer is – if you want to but be very aware of what it's going to tell the people who live in your town or see you driving.

Having signage on your vehicle is certainly a good brand awareness strategy, as long as it's done within your branding and complements what it is that you do and how you do it. Full car skins are very eye-catching and makes you acknowledge, even if subconsciously, that brand.

The big question is – what's your expected return on investment for doing the signage and will the signage give you that return on investment? If the answer is yes and yes and you can keep your car clean and on brand – go for it.

I've certainly done it for a business I've owned before and it worked amazingly well for brand awareness – especially because there were two vehicles driving around with the brand on it. I would probably do it again with no expectations other than using it as a brand awareness strategy.

Leveraging the power of referral marketing

Referral marketing is the practice of asking your happy, satisfied current (or past) customer if they know anyone else that would like to buy your products or services. Simple, right? Why do so many of us not do it then?

Side note: Referral marketing, although put in the classic marketing strategies section of this book, can 100% be a digital strategy too – and probably works even better using digital techniques.

The most common questions about referral marketing are:

- how do I ask someone for a referral?
- when do I ask someone for a referral?

Let's deal with the second question first. When do I ask for a referral? When your customer says to you, "thank you so much" or "this has been great" or "this is exactly what I needed" or "you've been fabulous, thank you" – THIS is the exact time to pipe up. You can say, "I am so happy you're happy. If you know of anyone else who needs something similar, sing out and let me know or tell them to come and see me."

Referral marketing can be much more than "Can you give me the name of a friend who'd like to buy, too?" You can have something as simple as "Don't keep us a secret" at the bottom of your email signature that nudges the reader to think differently about your email. It could be as simple as saying in an email, "Feel free to forward this email onto anyone in your world who you think would get value from it." Same goes for social media – asking followers to share the post with their friends and family on their own socials.

But the number one rule in referral marketing is to say THANK YOU to the person who made the connection between you and their friend or connection. The simple act of saying thank you, appreciating that your customer went above and beyond to help you in business, says more about your business and you than the product or service you sold them in the first place.

I really value referral marketing and take the attitude that "givers get". So, wherever I can, I make connections and referrals between my networks, and appreciate the thank you I get back. But I also hope that the favour will be returned at some stage and that will help my business grow, too.

Word-of-mouth marketing – an underrated marketing gem

Word-of-mouth marketing is a little like referral marketing – except you have less control over it. It's happening for you, often without you even knowing or asking for it.

Back in the pre-digital days of marketing, we'd say that if you do a great job for someone they would tell 10 people, if you do a horrible job, they will tell 100 people. Now in the digital age, it's more like a great job equals 100 people and a bad job equals 100,000 people. The word-of-mouth marketing we want is only good but the reality is that a bad review travels faster than a good one ever will.

Like referral marketing above, word-of-mouth marketing works both offline and online. Although it's in the classic marketing strategy section of this book, it's more viral in digital marketing than it ever was before digital was a thing.

How do you know if word-of-mouth marketing is working in your favour? Well, you have to ask. Ask a new customer or client how they found out about you? Simply ask – they will tell you.

The power of asking your clients quality questions like this is so underrated by business owners who are wondering where to spend their marketing dollars or if their marketing is working. Sometimes data from asking questions is all you need.

Word-of-mouth marketing can come from happy customers telling others in their world, someone who read your article published in the local paper or on a digital blog, someone who follows you on social media, someone who saw you on TV or heard you on the radio or someone who saw you in the supermarket last week and overheard you talking about your products or services.

Creating word-of-mouth marketing

- Do a sensational job at what it is that you do – surprise and delight your customers, give exceptional service and just be a good human.

- Create shareable content – whether that be an article with three tips or a video on how to use your product to make your customer's life better, easier, simpler or more meaningful.

- Again, say thank you to the person referring you, if you find out. It's a little easier to see who's sharing your posts on social media with their friends and family and thank them, than it is to say thank you to the lady who may or may not have overheard you in the supermarket and spread the word that way – but we are thankful for both.

The relevance of cold-calling today

Cold-calling is or was the act of calling someone who you've never met and perhaps hasn't heard of your brand or business.

It's the one marketing strategy that has an enormous "ick" factor in my mind and one that I would recommend to few business owners, if at all.

Does it work? Yep, it does. There are rooms full of direct market sellers right now dialing numbers to people they've never heard of to sell them things they didn't know they needed. If it didn't work, there would be no rooms full of people doing it.

Is it ethical? Mostly no, in my opinion and in the ways that I see it used.

Of course, these days it's just not about ringing someone on their phone, it's about connecting with someone on LinkedIn or Instagram and sending them sales messages.

Honestly, it's the best way to get blocked and deleted – both online and on my phone.

Marketing in the digital age is all about building relationships, building communities, earning the money you make through connections, providing extraordinary service and being the best you can be in business.

Cold-calling for me, is like going on a first date and proposing marriage over pre-dinner drinks – "Whoa there, Nelly, hold on, buddy, I need to get to know you a little first."

"

As a small business in the country, one of the best things you can do is watch what the "big end of town" does with marketing.

"

If you want to tap into an audience that you don't currently have access to, then think partnership and collaborations. Check out Tip #70.

So, cold-calling is a no, in my opinion. There are much better marketing strategies to put your effort, energy and money into than this.

> **BONUS TIP**
>
> Before I finish this section, another marketing no – never buy an email list and start emailing everyone on the list. It's just as ikky, if not more so and it's just not right for your brand.
>
> Protect your brand – it's all your business has.

The many benefits of a loyalty program

Loyalty programs have been around for many, many years. Way back in 1793 American retailers would give out copper coins to customers after their purchase – which their customers would use and redeem at their next purchase.

As a small business in the country, one of the best things you can do is watch what the "big end of town" does with marketing.

What do the businesses with the huge marketing budgets, with the rooms full of expert marketers, do with their marketing? Almost every big business, especially retailers, have loyalty programs. Why? Because they work.

In my Kitchenware Queens days, we had the Queens Club. How could I resist calling my loyalty club, the Queens Club? For every dollar spent, you earned one point – no rocket science there – and it was monitored by our POS system. Once they had 500 points (so had spent $500) they would get a $50 voucher to spend in store.

That equated to a 10% loss over time. So, did we think about our pricing strategy? Did we lose 10% on every sale? No, because before implementing the loyalty program, we put up our prices over time between 5 and 10 percent. We knew not everyone would reach 500 points and that not everyone was a part of our loyalty program. (Some people say no – heaven knows why.)

Those $50 vouchers were printed vouchers that were handwritten with a thank-you and sent out to those loyal customers once a month. A photo was taken of all the vouchers being sent out, in bright pink envelopes – 100% open rate, remember? Then that photo was shared across our socials. Guess what that drove? More traffic in store and more members into the Queens Club.

The Queens Club also had a birthday voucher attached to it and for your birthday, each member was given a $10 gift voucher to spend in store. Once an elderly lady come in and told me that our birthday voucher was the only gift she received on her birthday. I cried at that, and also thought – man, you just can't buy customer loyalty like that. (Or you can actually, with $10.) Our Queens Club was simple and effective.

Coffee shops do loyalty clubs exceptionally well with cards to buy nine coffees, get one free. Where are you going to get your coffee each day? There, of course. You want that free coffee, after all – that 10th one tastes better than the other nine, because it's for free.

Loyalty programs create loyalty. You might be thinking, *But, Jenn, I have so many cards, I often don't present them or forget about them.* You're right, you probably only use three out of the 25 you have – but who are those three and why do you use them?

There is something quite unique, special and different about a local small business in a country area having a loyalty program, as opposed to a big multi-national company.

Maybe you're not in retail, but a service-based business and you're wondering how you can have a loyalty program or if you should.

It is seven times more expensive to acquire a new customer than it is to get a current customer to come back and purchase from you one more time.

So there's a lot of scope to move when it comes to paying to implement a loyalty program or thinking about what margins you might lose if you have one.

Of course, from a marketing point of view, loyalty programs aren't just about creating loyalty with customers. They are also about collecting data which can help you build your business:

- you get to learn so much more about who your ideal customer is (invaluable research)

> **It is seven times more expensive to acquire a new customer than it is to get a current customer to come back and purchase from you one more time.**

- you identify your top-selling products or services
- you have a loyal email list you can market to with other goods and services
- you have built goodwill in your business
- you have a powerhouse of word-of-mouth referrers in your business.

CHALLENGE

If you don't have a loyalty program, please put it on the list to investigate how it could work for you and your customers. Think about the ones you use, why you use them, how it makes you feel and start there.

Bring back the lumpy mail

Lumpy mail is one of those classic marketing strategies that probably works better now than it did back before digital media. Lumpy mail is just that – mail that has a lump in it, although it doesn't have to have an actual lump to get the return you are after. Just like using snail mail and pink envelopes to get the 100% open rate, this is the goal with lumpy mail.

It's about doing marketing differently.

Who gets mail these days, either anything at all or mail that doesn't have a clear window (a bill)? Hardly anyone. Imagine getting a parcel or an envelope that is either pink or has a lump in it. Curiosity will kill the cat, right? You will open it purely to find out what's inside.

The catch, of course there's a catch, is that although you will get a 100% open rate, what is inside must be powerful enough and engaging enough to cause the recipient to take further action – buy this, do that, scan here and so on – act on your call to action.

Lumpy mail inspiration

The brightly coloured envelopes have worked best for me in the past. Here's some other ideas to give you some inspiration:

- **small bar of soap** – this is a cold-calling piece of mail – you don't know me from a bar of soap
- **gold-painted rock** – you might have struck gold – having fun with a serious topic
- **kitchen timer** – the time is now to purchase your new cookware
- **fridge magnet with cooking conversions on it** – this is measuring your cake success – for a cake decorating shop
- **stress balls in the shape of an aeroplane** – to fly high with success in leadership
- **tea-bag** – rest up and have a cuppa with me as you read
- **a key** – the key to success, life or happiness
- **calculator** – according to my calculations.

> **BONUS TIP**
> Head to Pinterest to be inspired with loads more ideas or ask ChatGPT.

Let's head back from the creative part of lumpy mail – aka the lump – to the why and the goals of such a marketing strategy. Having a goal and knowing what a successful campaign looks like is so important.

You do need a goal and a measure of success – just like in any other marketing strategy. The success isn't in the lump – it's the copy that goes in to it. The lump should relate in some way to the written copy that's with the lump – see the examples above.

The copy and entire project should be on brand for you – there's no use sending something that is so out of the box for you and doesn't align with your brand or isn't relatable for your audience. If I sent a golf ball with copy about a business mulligan – a second chance to perform an action, best known in golf – but none of my clients either understand this word or that it's a golf term, then it misses the mark. I'd be better off sending a kitchen timer with the copy – time's up for bad marketing – and a call to action to chat with me and sort out your marketing.

So, set goals. Set outcomes for success. Understand what the end goal is and start with the end in mind, come up with the lumpy mail concept and the action-driven copy to go with it, and then test and measure.

I love lumpy mail for all sorts of reasons – 99% open rates, brand awareness, personality marketing and of course, standing out from the crowd. It's one of the most under-utilised marketing strategies out there – because no-one thinks about snail mail any more.

What lumpy mail strategy can you think of for your business? What do you need more customers or clients to do? Remember, start with the end in mind.

Competitions as strategic marketing

Competitions are great for a variety of reasons. But it's important to know the reason why you are running a competition and what the end goal is.

Start with the end in mind. If you are using a competition to raise awareness of your brand – great – what does success look like? Raising brand awareness is certainly part of any good marketing strategy, but my bank manager doesn't accept awareness as payments. You need more than awareness or at least make sure that every other marketing strategy you have in place isn't for brand awareness also.

If you are doing it to list build – brilliant – love that. What are you going to do with that list once you have it? What's the marketing plan and strategy for that?

Competitions work really well when done in collaboration with other business owners who have your target audience too but aren't your competitors. But again, think about your end result.

The worst thing I see with running competitions is the business owner getting the prize wrong. For instance, an accounting firm runs a competition online and offline to win an iPad. Great prize, yes. For sure, I'll have a crack at that as I need a new iPad. But I don't need a new accountant – so I am only interested in the iPad. If the end goal of the competition for the accountant was to list build, then they have a list potentially full of people who are interested in the iPad, not in them.

Imagine if they had offered a free business assessment or an opportunity to win back the annual accountant fee or a free three-hours of financial advice. The number of people who entered would be significantly lower, but these people would be more likely to become future customers and that's a much better outcome for the business.

Be wary of your state government restrictions around competitions. In some states, you need to pay a fee for holding a competition or if the prize is valued over a certain amount, you have to declare it or apply for a permit or pay a fee – so do some research.

Online, be aware of the platform's restrictions around competitions. Facebook is very different to Instagram – check what you can and cannot ask people entering your competitions to do and what you need to declare in any posts on these platforms. We all ticked that box as we created our accounts and said we would follow the rules when we signed up to these platforms – we just didn't read the rules. So again, do some research.

Competitions should have a good quality prize that your ideal audience wants to get. The competitions should be short and sweet – really harnessing the power of urgency and scarcity marketing mentality:

- urgency – there's only three days to enter, so hurry
- scarcity – there's only one prize.

I have a checklist for running a competition and although the checklist is mainly around running one online – it's still a good checklist if you are running a hybrid competition – online and offline. Download it from the QR code at the back of the book.

The benefits of sponsoring events

Sponsoring events is a great way to build relationships in your community – but only if you do it right. Sponsoring events is another great brand awareness marketing strategy for getting your name out there – especially if you are new to business or new to town.

I would implore you to do your research. Make sure that the event you are sponsoring aligns with your business values and has an audience of customers you would like in your business.

Many of us small business owners sponsor local events like the local footy team, school fetes, the local lions club, netball club, tennis club, dancing studio and so on – there's a billion ways to get involved in sponsorship in your local area. But again, what's the goal? What do you want to get out of it as a business owner?

Is having your name read out to 20 grown men who have just played two hours of football and are completely exhausted really going to bring you sales or even brand awareness? Even if it's printed in the paper each week in tiny, tiny writing? Maybe it will and that's great. But maybe it won't, and you need to think outside the marketing square a little more and put a little more oomph behind your sponsorship to the local footy club.

Two ways that come to mind straightaway are:

1. You could make a trip to the footy a few times a year and cook the BBQ for the crowd attending. Wearing your brand or have a sign up – perhaps that could be part of your sponsorship package – even if you have to supply the sausages.

2. Perhaps it's not the footballers you support and sponsor but instead you give a sponsorship to Volunteer of the Week or Club Person of the Week. How much more cred and surprise and delight does that have for that person who turns up every week, helps out in their own time, and gets a thank-you for doing so from you and from their fellow club people? Now that's using sponsorship to your advantage and theirs – everyone looks good and gets warm fuzzies from what you've given.

I am sure you can think of more ways you can think differently about sponsorship.

Sponsorship rules

When I had a shop in the main street of my town, we had some rules around sponsorship – these might be useful to you.

- We only sponsored local events (with the exception of the Good Friday Appeal or maybe one or two others).
- We always gave vouchers – never products. We wanted that person to come into our store and have an experience, see what we had, and give us a chance to interact with them – you never know, they might just become a referrer of business for us.

- Everyone who wanted a donation had to fill out a Donation Request Form. You can download it by heading to the QR code at the back of the book. There were two reasons for the form:
  - what's in it for us – what marketing or brand awareness are we going to get from sponsoring your event?
  - if we're going to give up some of our profit to help you, you are going to have to work for it. Put some thought into your response and show us you're keen for a personal sponsor, rather than just thinking of us as another business to call.

Making a statement with billboards or blackboards

Putting your brand out there on a billboard is very old-school when it comes to marketing. It's probably now outside the realm of what most of us business owners can afford to do anyway.

But as always, I want you to think outside the square. It might not be the giant billboard outside the entrance to your town or the one that's on the CityLink road in your nearest capital city, but it might be the sandwich board one that's sitting outside your bricks and mortar store that says "Open".

If you do have one that sits outside your store front and it does say "Open", please go get it and put it inside for now. Your shop being open should be obvious.

Have you ever walked past a Spec Savers store and looked at their sandwich billboard out the front? If you have or next time you do, you will notice it has appointment times available for that day. So if you haven't got an appointment but think, "Gosh, I've been meaning to make one," you can look at the available times, and fit it in that day. It is a little piece of magic, because they clearly know their ideal client is well-meaning but busy and they need to make it simple. Plus for them, appointment vacancies mean less money and less profit for that day – win/win.

Think about how this could apply to you if you are a hairdresser or barber, beauty technician, optometrist, physio, doctor – if your business is appointment-based, this is 100% a marketing strategy that you should implement and one that will bring in sales.

If your business isn't appointment-based, then your board still needs to say more than open. Years ago, I would walk past a motel every morning which had a different motivational saying each day. I loved reading them and nowadays would probably take a photo of it and share it on my socials.

My good friend who owns a coffee shop encourages her customers to write up cool quotes on her blackboard and shares them on her socials – tagging the person who wrote it, who then proudly shares it as well. Great UGC (user generated content).

Otherwise, use a QR code that people can scan and get a little something – a little surprise, a message video of you saying hello, an invitation to come in or perhaps you have a daily special you could offer.

On my drive to Melbourne along the Hume Freeway, there's a great example of billboard marketing. The billboards are homemade and, honestly, are pretty crap but they do grab your attention. The billboards are positioned along the freeway as you drive close to Avenel and they advertise a local stall that's set up at the service station stop, selling jams, spreads and fresh produce. There are about 10 signs as you travel along, telling you where they are – "next turn left", what they sell – "jams and spreads". But the ones that makes me smile every time are the signs about bacon jam. So, travel with me here. You are speeding along at 110 kilometres per hour, reading signs saying, "next exit, get your honey, jam" and then you see one that says, "Bacon Jam". The next one says, "Bacon Jam???" and the next one, "Yes, Bacon Jam, seriously". By now if you aren't curious about what bacon jam is, you aren't reading the signs. I am positive people pull in just to see what bacon jam is, as well as to get petrol and use the toilets. The signs are compelling, and I smile every time I see them. Great marketing – it probably cost them $50 in signs and the petrol each day to put them out and collect them again.

So think small when it comes to billboards. If you don't have an A-frame billboard out the front of your business but now want one, check with your local council as they often have associated fees, as it's on their footpath.

Your business's first impression – signage

I know this won't apply to everyone who reads this book because so many of us are digital only these days, but if you do still have shop frontage, this one's for you.

Side note: If you are digital only, your shop frontage signage are things like your Facebook Cover Photo, your latest post, your website and so forth.

Signage out the front of your shop is a great marketing opportunity for you – and, well, something most people misunderstand. It is certainly about your business name and what you do (if that's not clear by the name) but it is also a great opportunity to show some of your brand personality.

Why do most people get it wrong? They just put their name up on the front of their shop. Think about some beautiful photography. Remember a picture paints a thousand words so what pictures or photos could you use to entice people to get to know you better, come into your business and scan your QR code on your signage?

Do you have a website? Is it on your signage or window? I was once asked to do an audit on a small retail business in a town in regional NSW. The business owner wanted more website traffic and to build the e-commerce side of her business because her store was located in a tiny NSW town and it wasn't sustainable only competing for local business – she wanted to build more. She'd been trying to get more traffic online but it wasn't working.

The first thing I noticed when I walked in was there was no evidence whatsoever of a website. Other than a tiny line on her business card at the counter, if you bothered to pick it up, there was no way you'd know while shopping there that she also had a website you could purchase from. It wasn't on her door or window or signs, it wasn't announced at the counter, it wasn't on your receipt or written on the bag you received after you purchased – it was nowhere to seen.

This is probably the best thing about getting an outsider to come into your business and take a look at what your goals are versus what you are doing now to achieve them. It's sometimes the obvious that is missing. Many of us small business owners are too close to our businesses and often miss some simple steps.

Signage is important. When thinking signage, don't just think about where you'll put it, font size, colours and so on, think about it as another marketing activity and think strategic.

> **BONUS TIP**
>
> When I had my retail store, we used some beautiful photography on our signs with photos from a few suppliers – and then we asked them to pay for it. So our signage was done for free. Yay for us. Again, think outside the box.

Engaging your community with a newsletter

Don't flick by just yet. Stick with me. Newsletters are a powerful way of nurturing your customers until they are ready to buy and buy again. They make a great communication channel with your past and potential purchasers. But you need to be consistent and do them often without always selling in them – no-one likes to be sold to all the time.

How often is often? That's a massive "how long is a piece of string" question. Somewhere between a few times a week and quarterly is the general answer. More than a few times a week is too much, quarterly is too long between drinks.

A newsletter and email marketing should be thought about slightly differently. We will deal with email marketing in Chapter 7 but for now, let's talk about newsletters.

Newsletters should be full of value. Yes, they can be about creating sales, but it's not so much in a direct way. There's no buy this and this and this now, it's more selling without selling.

Let me give you two examples of how I have used newsletters in my business. In my retail business, a kitchenware shop, our newsletter was one of our most important strategies for building a community of buyers who would buy from us over and over again.

Each week we would send out an e-newsletter. Each newsletter had three parts to it:

- **Part 1 – a product or a range of products.** Something new in store, something on special, or just something they needed.

- **Part 2 – a recipe.** This was something quick my customers (busy mums) could whip up for a dinner, lunch, dessert or kid's party.

- **Part 3 – a cooking tip.** A hint or tip that would make their life easier.

The formula worked well. Either the recipe or the cooking tip involved the product that was also in the newsletter. People opened that newsletter, I am sure, for the recipe or the cooking tip – the product was secondary. And they definitely didn't feel like they were being sold to by opening the newsletter. But they were. They were being sold to without being sold to.

Here's an example. One week the cooking tip invited customers to dip their wooden spoon into boiling hot water, and pull it out and smell it – the smell will indicate whether they needed a new wooden spoon or not. And guess what our product of the week was? Yep, that's right, our wooden spoon ranges. We sold out of wooden spoons that week. Customers brought in their stinky spoons to show us, they posted online their disgust that they were using their old spoons still and they shared our newsletter and corresponding social posts. (I am the repurposing queen and all elements from the newsletter went onto our socials eventually.) It was the big wooden spoon movement. Our brand reps commented on how many wooden spoons we ordered for weeks following that newsletter.

This is selling without selling.

Nowadays, in my marketing business, I use newsletters as more of a round-up of the month in my business. I share a round-up of my podcasts and blogs for the month (I produce four of each a month), I share podcasts I might have been a guest on (giving others a shout-out), and share published articles from other media that I have written and been featured in (because PR is such a big part of my marketing strategy). I might share a recipe, like at Easter or Christmas or just because I love it, I share some marketing insights or a favourite quote and explain why I am sharing it, and I share some stories and ask some questions.

So, in my retail business I did a newsletter every week, and in my marketing business, I do it once a month. Other businesses I work with do seasonal newsletters, and others do them twice a week. Your goals and audience will indicate how often you should use newsletters as part of your marketing strategy. But you should use them.

But my biggest piece of advice – if you do them, do them consistently. Don't start and stop and start and stop.

Marketing at your local cinema

To advertise in a big city cinema might be a little costly, but putting an ad up in your local cinema might fit into your budget.

Cinema advertising has been around as long as cinemas. Most of us are getting settled or don't arrive at the movie until 10 minutes after the start time, knowing we are simply missing the ads, but it is a captive audience – at least the ones that are watching.

You need to be super strategic if you are going to use some of your marketing dollars on local cinema advertising. It can't be something you knock up. It has to be compelling enough that the audience is still thinking about your ad, after they have watched the movie they went there to watch in the first place.

This type of marketing activity is similar to TV and radio. It has to be memorable, compelling and part of many touchpoints for your business.

The best ones are a collaboration between a few businesses or a business that has an activity. For example, the local coffee shop with a special or the local mini golf fun park advertising before the kids' movie in the school holidays.

I have to admit, it's not one that I have undertaken in my business, so I don't have any direct wisdom to share as far as results go. But if you can get the strategy right and perhaps even the movie right, it could have a positive result. Make sure you know what the result is that you are expecting and you can measure the success of it.

Tapping into your local gym community

Advertising at your local gym can come in many forms. First, you need to make sure your ideal client or customer actually is the type of person to go to the gym – otherwise, skip this one.

Marketing to gym people

- Wear your business name on your gym gear.
- Put up a flyer on the community board.
- Produce a piece of marketing for their televisions that are on rotation for the whole day among other ads.
- If your clients are definitely the people who go to the gym, chat to the owner about how you might collaborate together or do a marketing partnership. Every gym is always looking for more members, just like you are looking for more customers or clients – how can you make it a win-win? I discuss partnerships and collaborations later in Tip #70.

This marketing strategy is probably a little less obvious to us, because if you go to the gym, you just go. As a business owner, if you can think like a marketer, you will find endless opportunities you are already missing.

Using local community billboards in your marketing

Most towns and communities have some sort of community board. It's often found in the front foyer of supermarkets, at banks, on the front of shire or community halls or sometimes at the post office – especially if it's locally owned as opposed to corporate owned.

Many people use these billboards to sell things like dining room tables or couches. If your client or customer is the type of person who is likely to stop and read community billboards, then having a flyer up on them could create an opportunity for brand awareness and sales.

It is a very classic way of marketing and often forgotten about. Next time you are walking past one, stop, read what is on there and notice who is standing beside you too. They would work best when you have an activity happening in your business. Perhaps a sale, a VIP night, a come and try day, a special (free coffee with cake purchased), or if your business is about entertainment – the local cinema schedule, opening times for mini golf over the school holidays and so on.

Don't dismiss these opportunities because you think no-one reads them. You might not be your own ideal client and if you are looking for new marketing to try in your local town, this might be a good one to investigate further.

Investing in networking to grow

Your net worth is relative to your network. If you want more customers, more profit, more business, then building your network around you will present you with many opportunities to do it all. I can say, hand on heart, that my marketing business wouldn't be where it is today without the network that I have grown.

Now I am the first to say that networking in the past has not been my favourite activity. In fact, I would say that I have avoided many an opportunity in the past for networking, to my own detriment.

But over recent years (since I turned 40 – a few years ago now), I decided that putting myself out there more was the thing I could do to help grow my business. In the early days of networking, I would choose one person as soon as I got there – they would be my best friend by the end of the night (or for that day anyway). Or I would grab a plate of food and pass it round. Food gives you an "in" to any conversation, and people always love the person with the food. Just make sure they don't think you work there.

In more recent years, I have created and hosted networking nights, rather than networking myself. Networking is about brand awareness and people getting to know you. Everyone remembers the host, not just because they are the host, but they are also the person who's been emailing before and after the event and possibly the admin of the Facebook group now connected from the networking event.

"

To be a good networker is to be a good listener. If you are doing most of the talking, you are not networking properly.

"

To be a good networker is to be a good listener. If you are doing most of the talking, you are not networking properly.

If there are no networking events around where you live – create one. You can also do networking online as well – it doesn't all have to be face-to-face. I belong to a few amazing women's networks online. We meet for networking sessions, online lunches, learning sessions and more.

So, don't hold back with networking. Put yourself out there. You might need an elevator pitch – the pitch you give in the time you ride an elevator. For instance, when someone says, "Hey, what do you do?" To network well, you do need an answer to this question. Your pitch must be:

- memorable
- interesting
- succinct.

Make the person listening curious enough to ask a question or react in a positive way. Hopefully, they will say something like, "Oh wow – that's exactly what I've been looking for!"

Build trust with free samples

For the sake of this chapter, I am going to talk about freebies as tangible freebies – things you can actually hold, as opposed to digital downloads. I will chat about those when talking about lead magnets in Tip #97.

Giving away samples is an excellent way to either get new customers or get your existing customers to buy something from you that perhaps they wouldn't or don't normally buy. The beauty and food industries do this so well. You might always buy honey from a certain seller but they also make lip balms or infused honey jams which you never buy – you think of them as your honey supplier. But when buying one day, you are given a free sample of their lip balm – you try it and wowsers, now you are converted.

The cost of the freebie you have given away is minimal compared to the lifetime value of the customer you just converted to buy more than honey from you. From a profitability point of view, if you could get 35% of your customers to buy one more product every time they shopped with you, what would that equate to over 12 months?

This book isn't about numbers or finances, but these are the figures you should know in business. What's your client or customer worth to you each year and in the lifetime of them being your customer? If you know that, you can not only see the power of converting them into buying more often and buying more products, but perhaps you can see the entire reason for this book – the power of MARKETING.

Free samples can be given away in store, with every website order, through sponsorship of an event or function, just to name a few.

I recently attended an awards night, where I was awarded a "Woman to Watch" award. The sponsor was an up-and-coming beauty skincare brand. My prize included some samples of their products. Now, truth be told, they sat there for four months until I cleaned out my office one day. I did, at one point, throw them in the junk pile to go out, but had second thoughts, put them in the bathroom and used them. I was sold. On the first use of this tiny sample, I was sold. My skin felt incredible, and I think it looked it too.

I am now their customer. So far I have spent many hundreds of dollars on their products and will be a customer for a long time, I suspect. So, whatever the cost to sponsor that event, if there were 10 other people like me they converted in the room of a few hundred, the ROI (Return on Investment) was perfect. If they had just sponsored the event, with no samples given out, then they would not have found me as a client – it was the use of their samples that sold me, not their name branded all over the event marketing.

Not every business can have sample ranges, but if you can, invest in them. Know your numbers, know the real cost of the samples you give out but also understand the lifetime value of the customers you convert. For those of us who don't have samples, join me later to talk digital downloads and lead magnets – because that you can do and the results can be the same if done well.

For more on freebies and samples, read Tip #106.

The subtle power of the upsell

Upselling is certainly a marketing strategy that has been used since the dawn of trade. Upselling (as opposed to cross-selling – see next tip for cross-selling) is the process whereby you upsell into something bigger, brighter and if you are doing it correctly, more expensive.

Here's an example – you want to buy a car. You aren't really sure what car to buy, but you definitely want a car. You head to the car yard and find a fabulous salesperson who is willing to listen to what you need and ask good quality questions to understand what car is going to best suit your needs.

You decide on a Ford Everest, the car that will best suit you. But rather than the base model you had already decided on, you end up buying the mid-range model with the heated seats, sunroof and an app to download to start the car – even though you didn't want any of this stuff. That's an upsell. You wanted the Everest but now you are driving away in the mid-range model, not the base model.

Same with fry pans. Rather than buying the $20 one, you buy the $150 after chatting to the salesperson. Or you ask your new accountant to do your annual tax and you are sold into a package that includes doing your tax for five years, not just one.

The magic of upselling is in listening and asking quality questions. It's in knowing your products so well that you know what will best suit your customer or client. It's also understanding what level has the best profit margin for you and your business too and attempting to persuade the buyer to buy that version.

Think Good, Better, Best as a marketing model. If you sell services, what are your good, better and best offerings customers can buy from you? Or if you sell products – what's the good, better and best ranges?

Good, Better, Best is used over and over again as a marketing and sales strategy. Buy any online program and there's going to be a choice of at least three versions of the program. Take a look around you and start noticing the good, better and best ranges of products from tomato sauce in the supermarket to holiday flights around the world.

There is a science to it – if done correctly. It is basically the job of the good and best packages to sell the better one. The better one has the biggest profit margins and the biggest value for the buyer. There will always be customers who will never buy anything but the good range (budget) and same with the best range (status), but for all those undecided or wanting to upgrade, there's the better range. The ranges are often priced accordingly too.

Good might be $99, better might be $159 (but remember, less work, more profit and most value) and best is perhaps $500. What's the logical choice? Better, of course.

Spend some time looking at what you sell and how you can upsell your customers. Just like with the free sample chapter above, if you know your numbers then you know that if you can get your customers to buy 10% more from you each year, that it will increase your profit by x annually. Without chasing new clients, you can become more profitable by increasing the spend of those who already know, like and trust you.

And then the subtle art of cross-selling

Cross-selling is the process of selling your customers something in addition to what they already need or want to buy. Remember upselling is upselling what they are buying, cross-selling is adding to the sale.

Let's use the same examples from upselling – purchasing a car. Cross-selling when purchasing a car might be purchasing a special formula to protect the paint of the car, purchasing insurance for the car, floor mats or more warranty. You already have a warranty on your car (if it's new anyway) but they are cross-selling you into more.

Or with the frying pan example, you have purchased a frying pan for $150 but you also purchase a special brush to clean it, or the matching pots to go with it.

As for the accountant example, you've purchased a package for them to do your tax for five years but there's also offers for investment advice, a tax audit and so on – they are cross-selling you from one service only to many. All these examples are increasing the profit of your business.

The accountant example, in particular, increases the lifetime value of the client from a one-off to "we can't leave this firm because they are just too ingrained in my financial life."

Cross-sells don't always have to be used purely to increase profit in a sale. In retail, they are often used wisely to shift slow stock. The cross-sell item might have had a lower profit margin, but if the product isn't moving on its own, it needs to be teamed up with a product that does sell well to get it moving. Cross-selling in this instance is often done instead of discounting a product and it works well if the products that are being sold together work well together.

Let's say you have a dinner set that always sells. But the duck-egg blue mugs you purchased in bulk for a steal aren't moving at all. (There was probably a reason why they were a steal from the manufacturer.) So your marketing might be something like "buy this dinner set and received six mugs for an extra $10" or even for free, depending on your margins for both products. The customer wants the dinner set, they came to buy the dinner set, but for an extra $10, how could they resist?

CHALLENGE

Look around your store or look at the services you sell and rethink how you can cross-sell them together to create more value for your customer and more profit for you. After all, it's 7% more expensive to get a new customer than it is to upsell or cross sell to an existing customer or client.

Magazine advertising in the digital age

Magazines are having a renaissance in recent times. I have seen so many new, beautiful magazines coming out in recent years. Some are wholly digital (not printed) and some are a hybrid, digital and a limited print run. So, magazine advertising is making a comeback.

I am, of course, going to reiterate what I have said all throughout this book – you need to know your audience and know where they hang out to know if a particular marketing strategy is right for you and your business. Magazine advertising is no different. Do your clients/customers or ideal clients or customers read magazines? If yes, do they read digital or print ones or both? The answers to these two questions will help you decide if magazine advertising is for you.

The magazines out in recent years aren't your *Women's Weekly* or *Cleo* type ones but more niched with smaller readership numbers. But they do have a super committed and loyal audience who read and buy every edition.

Investing in magazine advertising

If you are going to advertise in a magazine because you know your customer or clients do read them, here are some tips for getting the most out of your investment.

- Write an article for the magazine as well as put in an advertisement. You know so much about your industry, so never underestimate what you know that others would like to know. You CAN 100% write an article for a magazine.

- Use professional photography, and at least one photo in the advert needs to be of YOU – yes, you the business owner. If there's no human relationship formed through photos, then you are simply an ad in a magazine. Your human-ness will make you stand out as the reader is flicking through the pages.

- Know what you want from the advert – what's the return on investment you are expecting? Any links used in the advert should be traceable and unique, so you can gauge how many people clicked the link or scanned the QR code.

- Make it memorable. Make it stand out from the crowd, do some research and find what you do and don't like in magazine ads. Find out, if possible, where in the magazine your ad will sit – near whose article and see if you can tailor your advert even more, given that information.

Don't dismiss magazine advertising in the digital age – they are coming of age too.

Pamphlets and brochures – far from extinct in modern marketing

Creating pamphlets and brochures for your business is similar to having a physical business card. You have to weigh up a few things:

- Your brand values – if one of your brand values is being environmentally conscious, then having 1000 brochures printed and either sitting in your office or thrown out after a quick read by a client might not serve you.

- What would your ideal client want – do they enjoy tangible things like brochures or would they prefer an attachment to an email? Remember business is not about you, it's about your client – so it doesn't matter what you prefer, it's their preference that should be considered in any decision.

- If you do decide to have something in print form, how can you make it more environmentally friendly?

Of course, the big question is FOR WHAT PURPOSE would you have one anyway? Marketing needs to be about strategic decisions and not just about "well, I've always printed a brochure." My mentor once told me how he saved his client $30K in their first session. They took out a full page in the Yellow Pages every year but when looking at the leads and data, they discovered that the ad really wasn't bringing in the business so they cancelled it. They'd always done that ad, so never really thought about it and whether it worked, the bill came and they paid it. Doing things in business "just because" is not a good strategy.

CHALLENGE

What do you do in your business without really thinking about it – you have always done it that way, so you just keeping doing it that way? Nothing changes if nothing changes ... Take a look through your marketing and ask yourself, *Do I need to still do this or produce that?*

For what purpose? This is the big question you need to answer here as you read this section.

- Who's the brochure for?
- Where do you use it?
- Can it be done better or differently or both?
- What's in the brochure?

Do you have a brochure or pamphlet in your business? Printed or digital? If you do, get it out and make a mental note of how many times you use the words "I" or "we". If your brochure is full of "I do this, I do that, I've done this for this many years" or "we do this, we offer that, we are that good because we" and so on, then walk to your nearest bin and throw the brochures out now. Or if they are digital, put them in your digital rubbish bin. Every time you use the word "I" or "we" you are talking about yourself and your customer or reader has officially lost interest around paragraph two. They've looked at all the pictures, read three seconds of it and it's likely in their bin or in a drawer where it will stay. Marketing has to be customer centric – not you centric. The customer does not care who you are, what you do or anything until they know that you can help solve their problem or surprise and delight them. As long as you are talking about yourself, you are not helping them, solving anything for them or delighting them.

It doesn't mean everything you are saying in the brochure is rubbish, it just means you need to say the same thing a different way. For instance, let's say your brochure has a section that is titled "What We Offer" and then some dot points. From a customer centric point of view and a reader's point of view (remember this is marketing and you are trying to convert a reader into a lead or a sale), you could say "What's in it for you" with probably very similar dot points. Can you see the difference? In the first example, you are talking AT your reader and talking about yourself – in the second one you are saying "I get you, I know how we can help you and here's how". Your reader feels heard and seen and you are likely to pass the "head nod test" here. The head nod test is exactly how it sounds, someone is reading your brochure and their head is nodding in agreement with what they are reading.

Offering a guarantee to build trust

We see big businesses using 100% back guarantees in their marketing and that's something that us small business owners in the country should adopt, where we can. The offer of a "100% money back guarantee" means the buyer has little to no risk in when making this purchase and for you, as the business owner, it says to any potential buyer, "I believe in my product or service so much, that I am prepared to offer you a 100% money back guarantee". It's a great way to set yourself apart from your competitors.

However, if you are going to offer one, then you have to stand by it. A buyer who is impressed that you offer a 100% money back guarantee might tell 10 of their friends. But if the product isn't what they wanted and they try to return it under the 100% money back guarantee and you make this anything but smooth and easy for the buyer, they will tell a few thousand people about it via social media.

Research does tell us that the number of people who actually return a product under a 100% money back guarantee is very small and the return is probably quite legitimate – so the risk to you as the business owner is small.

And, quite frankly, if someone buys a product from you, returns it, you make that return easy and simple for them, and they still aren't happy, then they are the most wonderfully perfect customer to give to your opposition – who wants clients or customers like that anyway?

Print marketing, old-school but still effective

In this section, I want to dive a little deeper in to print marketing. I've talked about newspapers, business cards, brochures and so forth already, but there is a whole other, enormous, category of print marketing that we need to discuss here. Think t-shirts, calendars, mugs, pens, drink bottles – the list is endless and they all fall under brand awareness marketing.

So, do they work and are they worth the investment? Now I know that you know what my answer is going to be and I also know you aren't going to like it. My answer – yes and no – and it depends. Here comes that question again – *for what purpose?*

In my retail days in the kitchenware shop, we printed calendars each year. We gave them away leading up to Christmas to our customers. Each year I pick up a calendar from my local Terry White Chemist, hang it in my house and look at their brand almost daily for 12 months. This is why I did my own calendar – it sounded like great brand awareness to me for very little cost per calendar. We invited customers to submit recipes, which were printed on each month – the customers whose recipes were printed beamed with pride. We asked our suppliers to sponsor a month which helped pay for most of the cost of printing. Did our strategy work? I think so. This is the issue with non-digital marketing – the results are not really that measurable, and there's a lot of "I think so" when looking at results versus costs. If I did something like that today, I would probably use QR codes and UTM links (UTMs are simple snippets of code that track performance of campaigns) so I could track how many people scanned the code and took the action I wanted them to take. This would help in measuring the success or otherwise of a campaign like this.

I think printed marketing has its place and I've seen some great examples of clever print marketing. You might just be reading one now – my book. It's a piece of print marketing – a massive investment of time, energy and money, but it is marketing. But other great examples are something as simple as printed bags for your store. We had bright pink candy stripe ones that stood out from the crowd when people carried them down the street. Remember how Coke had cans a few years back with people's names on them? They were part of their incredibly successful "Share a Coke" campaign. One of the best examples ever is the Ikea printed catalogue. It comes out once a year and for most households that's how long it stays on the coffee table.

Many highly successful print marketing campaigns are not exclusive to print but are run in conjunction with many other media forms – like TV, digital and so forth. Examples of this included Qantas's "I still call Australia home" campaign – they printed that on planes, played it on

TV and radio and had digital versions for us to watch, or one with a regional flavour – the Bundy Bear (drop bear) campaign. Their printed cartons of beer showed the brand's mascot, a bear, engaged in various humorous activities. The bear appeared on all sort of printed marketing materials and the campaign was successful in creating a strong brand identity and attracting a younger demographic to the brand.

So, print marketing can be very successful, often only if it's part of the overall marketing mix for that campaign.

The many benefits of joining your local chamber

I believe wholeheartedly – and the evidence backs me up here – that your net worth is relative to your network. So, as part of your marketing, join your local chamber or another organisation that has, possibly, both your ideal client and also some amazing collaboration partners to help build your business and get more leads or customers. Chambers are, in my experience, a dying organisation, but I really wish they were not. I've been involved in my local chambers since buying my first business 20 odd years ago. I've seen them, well mine anyway, at their peak and I have also been involved in the heart-wrenching decision to dissolve one too. Supporting the voice that supports small business has to be a good thing, doesn't it?

Local chamber marketing strategies

So, how is joining your local chamber a marketing strategy? It means:

- networking opportunities
- brand awareness opportunities
- mentor and mentee opportunities
- new leads, new clients or customers, new business
- new friendships (some of the best friends I have today I met through Chamber meetings and wine afterwards).

The whole purpose of this section of the book is to help you think outside the square with marketing. It's not just about posting on social media or sending an email, it's about getting your face out there, making connections, bringing more brand awareness to your business and networking. And in this case, joining your local chamber is the perfect storm for all this and more.

Joining a local chamber in the country is like joining the local CWA if you're a woman in the country – it just makes sense to support those who support your local community.

I urge you to be a chamber member and help your business grow alongside all members in your country community – it can only be a good thing.

Side note: If you're a country woman, make sure you're a part of your local CWA too.

Be you and share your story

Storytelling has been around for more centuries than we can comprehend. From the First Nations' rock paintings here in Australia to ancient Egyptian hieroglyphics – it is all about telling the story. I will go out on a limb here and say storytelling is one of the most missed pieces of marketing in most business owners' strategies or marketing.

Storytelling is powerful. People buy from people they know, like and trust, especially in the country.

In the country, if people don't know you or like you then they are probably never going to trust you and therefore buying from you will be a stretch, if they ever buy at all. To be able to like and trust someone, you have to know that person – that person needs to put themselves out there. Let people get to know who they are, what they do and why they do what they do. How do you do all that? Tell more stories.

If a client comes to me and says, "Jenn, I don't know what to post on social media – I'm out of ideas," my response will almost always be "tell a story" or tell more stories. As discussed in Tip #47, human to human marketing is the way to grow your business these days. Show up. Give. Be a human and sell some stuff.

> **Storytelling is powerful. People buy from people they know, like and trust, especially in the country.**

Your stories, your story, your why – these will all attract your customers. People who relate to your stories will like you and trust you. Simon Sinek once said, "People don't buy what you do, they buy why you do it." So, why do you do what you do? And once you've answered that, how have you gone about telling your clients, customers, prospects why you do what you do? Because once they know that, they know if you're the person who aligns with them and the person they should buy products or services from.

Caveat here: The stories you tell, the amount of personal information you give your audience, is one thousand percent up to you. You should only share what you feel comfortable in sharing. But you do have to share something – you can't say that I don't feel comfortable talking about myself and therefore I am not sharing anything. That's selfish. That's about you and the way you feel. Being in business is not about you, it's about your clients, your customers and they want to get to know the person behind the brand, behind the business.

You can start off by posting a photo of yourself in your business and write three things your clients don't know about you. Or you could do a video where you tell them three things they didn't know about you. This is a good start. What three things? Any three things you feel comfortable talking about. Why? So, your audience can get to know you, like you and trust you. So, you can build a relationship between you and your client or prospect and once that relationship is built, they are less likely to shop at your competitors or shop on price.

What would my three things be? I would say:

1. I don't like coffee – never had a coffee in my life.
2. I am a Justice of the Peace – from my days in law but now more about serving my community.
3. My last meal would be fairy floss. I LOVE my fairy floss, any colour but a little old and crunchy is my favourite.

Please show up for your community. Please tell stories in your marketing. Show up for your community at least a few times a week for a month, check your insights and analytics before you do it, make some notes of what they look like, and then reconcile the same data 30 days later. You will be super surprised with the result, I guarantee it.

Renting space and marketing in prime locations

Showing up in places your business isn't normally seen, or taking your business to town if you work from home or have a business run from your farm, can be a great way to attract new customers, get word-of-mouth going, have conversations with people who might not normally see your business and, of course, sell more stuff. Again, that's what we are in business for – to sell stuff and make money. This strategy will work really well if you are prepared to engage with people who walk by, have a set-up that creates curiosity with passersby and don't look like you are trying to sell me something I do not want. We all know how uncomfortable it is to walk past the people trying to convince us to give to charities or buy holiday vouchers.

I've seen this work fabulously with product-based businesses, especially the bespoke and unique small country businesses I get to work with. Their product sells itself – it is just a matter of getting in front of the people who didn't know they wanted this amazing product until they saw it.

It can also work well for businesses who are more service based. It's about creating conversations and no matter what you sell – product or service – while recognising that not everyone is your customer. Therefore, you don't need to talk to everyone (and look desperate as people walk by). If you and your business are good enough, you will naturally attract the right people to talk to.

Just one super hint – collect data. Whether you are selling a product and collecting money there or not, you need to ensure that you have the capacity to remarket to the people you are talking to or selling to, long after you have left that place or event. Collect emails and mobile numbers at a minimum, perhaps even postage addresses as well if that's going to fit with your marketing strategy. Of course, you'll need to give them a reason to give you that information, so check out the section on competitions and giveaways in this book to get some notes on those possibilities.

***

Here are my final thoughts on classic marketing strategies:

- You have to know your ideal client and whether a particular marketing strategy is likely to turn them into a paying client or customer. After all, that's the game – we are in business to make money. If the answer to this is no, then don't do it. Simple.

- And if it does turn them into paying customers, what is the cost? Think about the return on your investment. Is the strategy you are planning the best use of your money? Will it give you a profitable return?

- All marketing, no matter what strategy or what tactic, will work better when used in a campaign of many touchpoints. For example, simply printing a mug or having a business card is not going to change your business (or is unlikely to in the short term) but when it's part of a larger campaign that involves many touchpoints, tactics and strategies, then the mug or business card will work. Think of it like a cog in a wheel, maybe in a gearbox or in your Cartier watch – one single part doesn't make it work as it takes all parts working seamlessly together to create the product you use.

Chapter 4

THE ONE PERCENTERS THAT CAN HELP YOU BE A BETTER MARKETER

If you want to be engaging, be engaged.

—

Tracy Sheen, The Digital Guide, Toowoomba, Queensland

T his chapter is all about the one-percenters – those little things that you can do in your business today to help you be a better marketer. The things that might take 10 minutes a month to implement but can have a positive effect on your ability to market to your ideal client and add another touchpoint to your marketing strategy. Some of these things you are already doing, you're just not thinking of them as a marketing opportunity.

Invoices – more than just payment requests

If you are in business, then there is every possibility you send out invoices for payment to customers. But how are you using your invoices as a marketing tool?

There are several ways you can use your invoices as a marketing tool and depending on whether you email all your invoices or send them via the post, some suggestions below might work, some might not. But all are worth considering.

Most of us are using some sort of computer software to generate our invoices. For example, I use Xero and have used Quickbooks and MYOB in the past. These software programs have a space within the invoice for a personal note. There is often only one or two lines for the actual invoice – the rest is free marketing white space. In the past, I have put messages in my invoices about new product launches, I've introduced a new staff member, I've given cooking tips or enclosed a recipe (this worked well heading into Christmas where I shared my family's 100-year-old plum pudding recipe). I have even told some really bad Dad jokes when invoices have gone out around Father's Day.

This strategy lives somewhere between human-to-human marketing (showing personality with jokes and sharing something of value with a recipe) and a sales strategy (launch of a new product line or service), or just bringing joy in the hope that they might pay their bill faster by making them smile with a really bad Dad joke. Statistically, businesses are taking up to 120 days to pay invoices to some small businesses, according to data from Amex. Adding some personality or something a little extra into the mix to build a relationship with the person paying, or all the people it passes through beforehand, can only help to get my bills paid earlier.

Take a look at your software and see where you can put messages, share stories or add to the invoice. Look at your calendar and see what's coming up and what might make your boring "pay me" invoice into a personality branding piece of marketing.

BONUS TIP

If you send invoices via the mail, are you using the envelope as a marketing tool?

Marketing in your email signature

How many emails do you send a week or a month? I am guessing loads – am I right? Does your email signature form part of your marketing strategy? If not, why not? You are emailing people all the time and these people are either your ideal client or could know someone who is. Without your email signature being worthy of noting or sharing, it is definitely a missed opportunity.

At the moment, my email signature points to my podcast with the call to action of "listen in to the Small Business Made Simple Podcast", asks people to join my private Facebook Group, Like Minded Business Owners, and also has a link to book a discovery call with me if they need help with their marketing strategy. By the time you see it though, it should 100% have a link to read my book! It's bright, it's branded and it is definitely a touchpoint in my overall marketing.

Think about where you would like to send people who click a link in your email signature. Think about what the next obvious step is for someone to take after they read your email and see your email signature, for example, book a call, read a blog, engage with a social media post (don't write follow me on Instagram or Facebook – that's not a strong enough call to action so be more strategic than that), hit reply and connect or ring this number for something specific. You decide. But make your email signature a one-percenter that helps build your brand, get noticed, bring in leads and ultimately, bring in sales and profit.

I had a designer design my email signature – so reach out to your local graphic designer and see what they can produce. Or head to my favourite platform www.canva.com.au and use a template from there. But honestly, consider investing money into a professional design rather than investing your time into a template when it's not your zone of genius.

> **CHALLENGE**
> Create an email signature for your business that's worthy of taking notice of. Add your photo, and think about how you can deepen your relationship with the reader of the email and put that call-to-action in your signature.

Packaging, your silent ambassador

Packaging is like invoices – if you are sending packages in the mail, how are you using them to market your business? Packages are touched and handled by many more people than an invoice sent via email, so you have the opportunity to put your brand in front of many new faces who might be or might know your ideal client.

Self-branded packaging can be a little more costly, but how much more costly really? You are already paying for packaging, how much more would it cost to have a box or bag branded in your colours with your business name, logo, website and call to action printed on it?

If that's not an option, then consider these ones:

- organise stickers or sticky tape with your business name, logo, call to action printed on it
- order a personalised stamp and stamp your details and call to action on your packaging.

Or cheaper again, spend time handwriting a message to your customer, the postie or just the world on the outside. Many years ago when I used to write to my pen pal, we would always put funny messages on the outside of our envelopes for the postie to read. I'm not sure I ever got my mail delivered more quickly, but I am sure it would have made some posties smile that day. But packaging isn't just about the outside, it's about the inside too. What marketing messages are you sending when people open your packaging? Is there a handwritten note from you saying thank you or instructions on how to use or take care of the product, is there an upsell or cross-sell for next time, is there a sample of a new product (or just a different product), a gift voucher or discount voucher for next time? The list goes on but my point is – where are you missing marketing opportunities when it comes to packaging your products?

Wearing your marketing (uniforms)

If you're in business, you either employ yourself or some other incredible humans to help you build your business. Do you or do they have a uniform? If not, can they? If so, what marketing message is that uniform sending to the wider world and to your clients or customers who come to your work?

I saw a super cool t-shirt the other day worn by an employee of a multi-national environmentally conscious business which had a QR code printed on the back of it. I had followed the person down the street and saw the t-shirt and thought, *what a cool idea*. Did I scan it? I certainly did! The QR code went to their website, which was a missed opportunity – they could have made it so much more personal but the idea was great. They got another hit from me on their website that day and now their remarketing ads are following me around the internet – job well done on that marketing.

Your business name printed on your uniforms can help with brand awareness of your business. If you can take it to the next level and get someone to see the uniform and take another action, like visit your website or search you on socials or Google, then that's even better for staying in touch, especially if you have remarketing ads in place.

Making your website your digital storefront

Having a website is a crucial element of a comprehensive marketing strategy. Your website serves as the digital hub of your business, acting as a virtual storefront that's open 24/7. It plays a vital role in various aspects of your marketing efforts and yet I am asked, more often than you think, "Do I need a website?" My answer is almost always yes, absolutely you do.

In this digital age, you are expected to have some sort of Google presence – some sort of website that is your own piece of internet land. I often talk about not building empires on crown land. If you have only social media platforms as your storefronts, then you are one hundred percent building your empire on crown land – you are building your business on property you don't own and you have no control over it. You could be hacked tomorrow on Facebook, for example, someone could force your account to disappear and take all your business with them.

A website is essential.

This doesn't mean that you need to spend thousands on one. You could create a free Google Business profile website, if that's all you need.

> **BONUS TIP**
>
> Use your Google Business Profile like a Social Media Platform. Add photos to it, add posts to it, nuture it and get some good google juice from it.

If you have a business but nothing to show for it other than a social media presence, you are playing with fire. I will go out on a limb and say, your credibility as a business is being affected as well. People trust the web more than they trust a social media platform.

Your website is often the first touchpoint for potential customers. It's where they learn about your brand, products and values. A well-designed website creates a positive first impression (according

" A website is essential. "

to Forbes Advisor, a website visitor forms an opinion about your website in 0.05 seconds), establishes brand credibility, and helps shape your business's online identity. Your website is the go-to place for detailed information about your products, services, pricing and business story. It's like a digital brochure that customers can access anytime, anywhere.

Through your website, you can capture leads by encouraging visitors to subscribe to newsletters, download resources or fill out contact forms. These leads can then be nurtured through targeted marketing campaigns. A properly optimised website can improve your search engine rankings, making it easier for potential customers to find you when they're searching for products or services related to your business.

Having a blog or resource section on your website allows you to share valuable content that positions you as an industry expert and sets you apart from your competitors. This content can be shared on social media, boosting your authority and driving traffic back to your site.

If you sell products online, an e-commerce website enables customers to browse, select, and purchase items conveniently. It expands your market reach beyond your physical location. Interactive features like comments, reviews and forums encourage customer engagement and community building. This fosters a sense of connection and loyalty.

One of the best things about having your own website from a digital marketing point of view is having access to tools like Google Analytics, enabling you to track visitor behaviour, traffic sources and engagement metrics. This data helps you understand what's working and where you can improve your business. Being able to make strategic decisions based on data is invaluable to small businesses these days.

I would recommend that your website needs a big branding update every few years to keep it fresh and give your customers a better user experience. Websites are not a "done once" marketing activity. They need investment, time and energy because they are, at times, one of the first touchpoints for your potential customers. You need to incorporate a user-friendly design, clear navigation and relevant content, so your website becomes a pivotal tool in building a strong online presence and driving your business's success.

Activating social sharing and Pinterest pins on your website

This is another one of those one-percenters that just might help your content go further and reach more ideal clients. For most websites, the social sharing icons and the "Pin It" icon are pretty simple to set up – if you're not sure, check with your website developer.

If you're not sure what the social share icons are or what they are about, let me explain. When someone comes to your website to read your latest blog or look at a product, they might want to share that blog or product on to their social media platforms. With social sharing icons enabled, they simply click the social sharing icon they want such as Facebook. Their Facebook will open up with a direct link to your blog, so they can add their comments to your post and then click post. This makes sharing your blog or products a seamless and painless experience for your website visitor.

Making it easy for your website visitor to share your content increases the potential reach of your content, attracts new website visitors and provides social proof of the value and credibility of your content. And, importantly, social sharing icons mean that your website visitor doesn't have to leave your website to share your content. We all know and understand that once someone leaves your website for social media, there's every chance they'll fall down a content rabbit hole on that platform and might never make it back to your website. In fact, according to HubSpot, less than 30% of traffic will return to your website from social media.

Overall, including social sharing icons on your website can be a simple and effective way to increase the visibility and engagement of your content.

Crafting a converting 404 page

A 404 web page, commonly known as a "404 error" or "404 page not found" is a standard HTTP response code that indicates a server could not find the requested resource or web page. So if the website page you have typed into your browser can't be found or doesn't exist, a 404 error page flicks up onto your screen.

Sounds like a bummer, doesn't it? If it's your website, you really don't want this happening. But it does. Broken links, missing pages, old links in old search results – we can't be over it all. But the 404 error can be a great little marketing tactic. Because a 404 page can be customised by you, it is no longer a lost opportunity of website traffic because the page is no longer a dead end to content.

Custom 404 pages can be designed creatively and can serve as a way to engage users, provide assistance or showcase a website's personality even when encountering a missing page. Proper handling of 404 errors is essential for user experience, as it helps visitors navigate a website effectively and understand why they couldn't access the requested content. Additionally, it is crucial for search engine optimisation (SEO) purposes, as search engines prefer websites that handle errors gracefully and provide meaningful (customised) 404 pages.

You could customise your 404 page to direct them to a new freebie, to your podcast or blog pages, to a sales page, to the home page. You can make a bit of a joke out of the fact that they have found your 404 page, even if they didn't mean to.

Great uses for 404 pages

- **Lego:** Lego's 404 page features a playful and interactive experience where visitors are greeted by a cute Lego character apologising for the missing page. Users can then use virtual Lego bricks to build their own creations.
- **Airbnb:** Airbnb's 404 page uses humour to engage users. It shows a photograph of a remote cabin in the woods with the message "This cabin is off the grid... just like this page." The page also includes navigation links and a search bar to help users find what they're looking for.
- **HubSpot:** HubSpot's 404 page takes a humorous approach, displaying a search bar with the text "Sorry, this page is out of reach" and a CTA button that reads "Beam Me Up, Scotty!" It aligns

with the brand's inbound marketing theme and provides a quick way for users to return to the homepage.

- **Mailchimp:** Mailchimp's 404 page features an adorable image of a monkey scratching its head, accompanied by a humorous and empathetic message, "This isn't the page you're looking for." The page also provides links to the homepage and support center.

Remember that a successful custom 404 page should:

- be visually appealing and align with the website's branding
- clearly indicate the error and offer an apology or a humorous message to ease frustration
- provide a search bar or navigation links to help users find what they were looking for
- offer a way for users to get back to the homepage easily
- use interactive elements or engaging content to keep users entertained while they figure out their next step.

Custom 404 pages turn a frustrating customer experience into a positive and sometimes memorable experience. Now that is pretty cool.

The power of online directories

Online directories have been around as long as the internet, and one of your earlier memories of online directories might be the Yellow Pages or True Local. Online directories are important in today's digital age, because online visibility plays a crucial role in the success of any small local business. While social media and search engine optimisation are often at the forefront of digital marketing strategies, online directories are another valuable avenue that can significantly enhance your business's exposure and traction. These platforms not only provide a means for potential customers to find your business but also improve your local SEO and credibility.

Online directories are platforms that list businesses, categorised by industry and location, making it easier for consumers to find the services or products they need. They are often free to be a part of but can also be like a paid membership.

Leveraging these directories can offer several benefits:

- increased online visibility
- enhanced local SEO
- being present on well-known online directories lends credibility and trust to your business
- many online directories allow you to list your business in specific categories or niches.

Top online directories for Australian small businesses

- Yellow Pages
- True Local
- Google My Business
- Yelp
- LocalSearch
- StartLocal
- Hotfrog.

So, if your business is listed on any of these platforms, here are some tips for optimising your business:

- Ensure that your business details (name, address, phone number, website) are current and consistent across all directories.
- Fill out your profiles with accurate and detailed information about your business. Use high-quality images to showcase your products or services.
- Incorporate relevant keywords in your descriptions and titles to improve your chances of appearing in relevant searches.
- Respond to customer reviews, both positive and negative, to show that you value customer feedback and are committed to improving your business.
- Keep your listings up to date with any changes in business hours, services or contact information.

Online directories offer a cost-effective way for you to enhance your online presence, increase credibility and attract more customers. By strategically listing your business on reputable platforms, you can tap into a broader audience and establish a stronger foothold in your local market.

CHALLENGE

Go to Google, open an incognitio page and Google your business. Do any of the search results appear within directories? If so, go and make sure the information is up to date and make any changes necessary.

***

So these are your one-percenters, the little things you can add to what you are already doing. Their impact might not be immediate or fast paced, but you do these activities anyway, so why not put your marketing hat on and make them part of that top-of-mind marketing plan you do day to day, week to week or month to month?

Chapter 5

OUTSIDE THE MARKETING BOX THINKING

Small business can be an intense blurring of work and life. Clearly defining and communicating your boundaries can help balance both in a way that works for you.

—

Lee Longmire, Lee Longmire & Co
Narrandera, NSW

We are all doing business in an extremely competitive and very noisy marketplace. Whether your competition is the store down the road, elsewhere in your region, online or that big multinational that has come to town, we all have competition. Sometimes I feel like we are yelling into a black hole – no-one really sees us or hears our message. Obviously, some people are. But we keep thinking, "If I could just get more people to buy more often … then my business would be more profitable, I'd be able to take off more time, I would be able to …"

So, thinking outside the marketing box is an exciting chapter. I have run my business a little like "when they zig, I zag". It doesn't always pay off, sometimes riding the wave of the latest trend is how you get seen and get more clients or customers. Other times, it is about being ahead of the curve or simply creating your own curve. Creating your own path, your own curve is what this chapter will help you focus on.

Nothing changes if nothing changes.

So if you are stuck in a hole, reached your glass ceiling or need a marketing challenge, enjoy reading through my ideas for outside the marketing box thinking.

Align yourself with a charity – marketing with a cause

This is not about giving to a charity. It's not about donating to a charity. It is very strategic and if you don't like the idea of aligning yourself and your business with a charity to make more money, to bring more brand awareness to your business, then perhaps skip this tip. I make no bones about it – this is a strategy to help build your business. Be charitable about it, absolutely, but it is about business.

Let me start with how I aligned myself with a charity to grow my business. Perhaps after my story, you might see that you can be a very community-orientated and charitable person while building your business.

> **Nothing changes if nothing changes.**

I come from a smallish town, probably like you, and we have a few multi-nationals but not many (although more seem to be moving into the area each year). At Christmas, our Target Country (as it was then) organised the Wishing Tree. You've probably seen it – it's the tree they have in the front of the store that you can place gifts under for children and adults who might not be able to afford gifts for their families. But a chance conversation with a community health nurse brought to my attention that those gifts did not stay locally. As someone who always contributed significantly to those trees, I didn't think that was either right or well known. Did our local people know that they weren't necessarily helping their own local people?

Solution? Start one myself or ourselves, because my business partner was instrumental in pulling it off too – thanks, Jo Jo. We contacted the local community health organisation, said that we'd like to do a wishing tree in our store for locals who find it hard at this time of the year, but didn't know who these people were. Our question was – if we collected the toys and gifts, could they distribute them? The answer was a resounding YES. So we set up a tree, started marketing it and people came and brought gifts in.

So, what was the point? I did say it was a business decision as much as a decision to help others. The point was the exposure that wishing tree gave us. The point was that a person who had never been into my shop came in with a gift to put under the tree. The point was that we got to have conversations with people we'd never had conversations with before. Although they didn't purchase from us that day, we had the opportunity to build a relationship with them – not based on a transaction but based on community.

I want to share with you one of those moments that happened because of the wishing tree, that I'll never forget. A local lady walked in with a couple of bikes, scooters and helmets. And I cried. In fact, I am crying again, writing this in my book. You see when I was young, that lady would have needed those gifts under that tree for her family. That lady belonged to the "poor" family at my school. And here she was many years later giving back, or as the campaign was called, Paying it Forward. She doesn't know the impact that act had on me, but all these years later, it still makes me emotional. Christmas is magical.

So, back to the align yourself with a charity idea. You can see that it can work well for your business if you do it with intention. Maybe it's not a Pay it Forward wishing tree that you can do, but perhaps it's as simple as a raffle you host and sell tickets for in your shop. But if you align yourself with a charity for the purposes of helping your business, you need to make sure it creates traffic, conversation and community.

Host an event to build community and brand

Events take energy. There's no doubt about that. And they are definitely out of the box thinking when it comes to marketing.

Simple ideas for events might include product demonstrations for the products you sell. The demonstration could be by you or your staff or even the sales representative who sells the brand you are promoting. I am definitely one for putting it back on the brand for some help – like prizes or gifts, for example. You could do a whole town event like a VIP Shopping Night or you could host a retreat (see Tip #101) or you could host an evening event because you have a new range or service.

Planning an event

If you are planning to do an event as a marketing strategy for your business, then here are some tips on avoiding any tears leading up to the event:

- Plan, plan and plan some more! You can't be surprised this is my first tip – it's just so important. Along with planning, answer these questions:
  - What's the purpose of the event?
  - What kind of event do I want to hold? For example, networking, sales event, party?
  - What do I want the people coming along to the event to get out of it?
  - What do I want my business to get out of it?
  - What is my event budget?

- Don't do the event alone, if you can help it. Can you involve staff, friends, family, suppliers?
- What's your Plan B? You might not always need a plan B, but if Covid-19, floods, droughts, mouse plagues and unpredicted weather events have taught us anything, it's that a good plan B is a good idea.
- Have a run sheet which is essentially a play-by-play of your event. A run sheet breaks time into minutes or hours and has the tasks required to be done on it. These tasks might be before, during and after the event.
- If you can, giving back to your community would be my final tip – see Tip #66. It could be as simple as a gold coin donation that goes to a local charity or it could be a raffle prize or a silent auction – again, think outside the marketing box.

With some strategic planning, an awesome team by your side, a backup plan or two up your sleeve and a well-thought-out running sheet, you'll be running the show like a boss.

Showcasing at tradeshows and exhibits

Tradeshows or exhibitions are big. They often cost lots of dollars, take up loads of resources and energy and for most businesses, do not offer the return they should. But that lack of ROI (return on investment) is because the person exhibiting didn't plan and set achievable goals rather than the fact that their target audience wasn't at the event. Most of us are smart enough to work out if an event has our people at it or not. Where we fall down is the planning – pre-exhibiting, exhibiting and post-exhibiting bits.

Whether you are planning to exhibit at your local wedding exhibit, a wine tasting event, a tradeshow in your capital city or just at your local monthly market, there are some rules to follow.

Exhibit timing

Before the exhibit:

- Identify and prioritise the top three reasons why you're exhibiting. You may be exhibiting to:
  - gather qualified sales leads
  - make more sales
  - get in front of a new audience who needs to know what you do and how you do it
  - promote new products
  - get more brand awareness for your business
  - educate your audience with "how to" displays
  - perform competitive/market research.

  Whatever your reason, make sure you focus on these reasons when making your strategic and spending decisions:
- Set strategic, measurable show goals.
- Identify the products or services you'll showcase.
- Design an attractive, functional, uncluttered exhibit.
- Prepare your exhibit staff for show business.

During the exhibit:

- Have a clear concise message and stick to it. Remember *a confused buyer doesn't buy* and when at a tradeshow or an exhibit, competition will usually be fierce.
- Use high-impact graphics focusing on your prospects' needs.
- Record all critical follow-up information on a lead form.
- Talk to strangers.
- Remember to be present!
- Talk to other exhibitors.
- Leave the selling for the office, and network while you can.
- Have fun.

After the exhibit:

- Provide promised follow-up within 48 hours of show close (if not sooner).

- Also, make some notes, while it's fresh in your head, of what worked, what you could have done better and what didn't work for next time you exhibit.

- Industry statistics say that no follow-up is done on 80% of show leads! Prepare your post-show follow-up process before you even attend the show. Stand out by contacting your prospects by the agreed-to method – and no later than 48 hours after the show closed.

Teach your staff marketing

Do you have staff or contractors? How much do they know about marketing your business? Perhaps you should give them a copy of this book with marked pages so they can learn a little more about marketing.

I don't have staff at this point in my business. It's not my business model. I only have contractors. But when I did have staff for the first time, I learnt a massive lesson when we held our first staff meeting. The meeting was to help them see where the business was going and what was coming up. I thought it would be about my business partner and I talking to them. But I soon found out, to my complete and ignorant surprise, that once we started talking about marketing and things we wanted to do, our staff had amazing input and loads of ideas too. I am highly embarrassed that I hadn't given them a chance prior to this to help with marketing or business goal ideas, because they were brilliant.

What training, specifically around marketing, are you giving your staff access to? Are you talking to them about what it might mean to your business if they shared some posts from your business page to their personal page on Facebook, or shared your Instagram post on their stories or forwarded an email to a friend or family member?

Having them understand what marketing is, and see what impact they can have on the business – a business they, hopefully, love working for and want to see succeed, could lead to not only more sales but better employees, because everyone wants to feel a part of something. That something for them, could be your business.

There is so much power in teaching your staff about marketing and how to market – especially if you subscribe to the fact that *marketing is everything*. It's the way you answer the phone, greet customers, respond to that email, social media post or bad review. Teaching your staff about marketing not only takes the pressure off you to be the marketer but also future proofs your business.

Enrol them in some programs, share programs you have purchased with them, share this book with them or buy them their own copy. Tom O'Toole, a famous baker over my way and owner of the extremely successful Beechworth Bakery businesses, was once asked, "What if I train my staff and they leave? That's a waste of my money and resources." His response was, "What if you don't and they stay?" It will take some extra time, energy, money and resources to teach your staff about marketing, but imagine what it could do for your business. And if you don't, well, imagine that too.

The power of partnerships and collaborations

Both partnerships and collaborations are vitally important. These two "out of the marketing box thinking" strategies could change your business forever.

A partnership is when two or more individuals or businesses come together to work jointly towards a common goal. It's like joining forces to combine skills, resources and efforts, including marketing efforts. In a partnership, all parties share the responsibilities, risks and rewards of the business. Partnerships often involve legal agreements that outline the terms of the partnership, including profit sharing, decision-making processes, and the duration of the partnership. They don't always have to be this complex – it depends, unsurprisingly, on the goal of the partnership.

A collaboration is when individuals or businesses work together on a specific project or task while maintaining their independence. It's like a teamwork approach where each party contributes their expertise, ideas or resources to achieve a shared objective. Collaboration can be a one-time or ongoing arrangement, and it allows participants to leverage their strengths and skills without entering into a formal partnership.

The main difference between partnership and collaboration lies in the level of commitment and shared responsibility. In a partnership, there is a deeper and more formal commitment, often involving legal agreements, shared profits and decision-making authority. Collaboration, on the other hand, is more flexible and can vary in intensity and duration, focusing on achieving a specific goal without necessarily establishing a long-term commitment or sharing profits.

The idea behind both is to build your business and therefore the number one thing any prospective partner or collaborator has to have is – the same audience as you and not be your direct competition.

Examples of great partnerships you might know but may not have thought about them as business partnerships include Nike and Michael Jordan (watch the movie *Air*, it's fabulous), Apple and IBM (way back in 2014), Coke and McDonalds, Pepsi and KFC.

Examples of well-known collaborations – NASA and SpaceX (SpaceX belongs to Elon Musk), Telstra and Ericsson to develop and launch 5G and Red Bull and Go-Pro.

Collaborations have been very valuable in my businesses – all of them. When I ran a property law business, we collaborated with other local professional businesses. In my retail business, we collaborated with other businesses to host VIP nights and other events. In my marketing business I collaborate with other businesses doing Instagram Lives or takeovers, other podcasters or other businesses to do retreats with and of course my podcast, as I am always collaborating with guests.

We held a Christmas VIP night in my retail days, where we collaborated with 10 or so other businesses in the main street and opened our doors late. We shared email addresses, SMS numbers, social media platforms and snail mail addresses for marketing purposes. It was the second-busiest day of the year for us, only trumped by Christmas Eve. It literally brought in tens of thousands of dollars to our business in one night.

Who could you partner with or collaborate with, who has the same audience as you, but is not your direct competition?

Collaborations, especially, helped me build my business to the point that I could sell it in three days. If you don't do collaborations or partnerships at the moment, this is definitely one to start exploring.

> **CHALLENGE**
> Start a list of business owners you could approach to do a partnership or collaboration with. Reach out to them and ask if they are keen too. Sometimes these activities need leaders, so don't wait for someone to ask you, ask them!

Create a direct and effective SMS marketing strategy

SMS marketing is used sparingly in Australia at this point in time. There are times of the year such as Christmas, End of Financial Year and Black Friday sale times when we might find our phones pinging with SMS marketing messages but in general, we don't get many of them. In the US, however, SMS marketing is prolific.

I am pro SMS marketing but it must be used sparingly. When I had the retail business, we would use SMS marketing to remind people that our VIP Night was on tomorrow or in two hours (because we know how busy our customers are and they probably needed a nudge reminder). SMS marketing is good for time sensitive marketing activities.

However, I am not an advocate for SMS replacing email, for instance. If you send as many SMS messages to a client as you do emails, they might quickly become a foe rather than a friend.

The number one rule with SMS marketing is there has to be an opt-out available. If you are using your own phone to send marketing messages, you must include something like "text STOP if you want to opt out from these messages" and then you have to ensure you do stop. It's the law. Using an SMS company or if SMS is available through your email system is a much safer option. SMS marketing through channels like these is not free, so there will be a small fee per SMS. Of course, it goes without saying that before you message anyone at all, you have their consent to do so. Being on your email list isn't consent enough, it has to be specific consent to receive SMS messaging from you.

Using SMS marketing probably means that you will get a high open rate. We all live with our phones not too far away and get a high from the ping that someone has messaged us.

SMS marketing ideas

- **Segment your list** – make sure you send messages to the relevant part of your list. Consider segmenting demographics, behaviours and preferences, for instance.

- **Craft short clear messages** – SMS messages have character limits, so there's no room for waffle.

- **Always include a call-to-action in the message.** In other words, they have read it, and now what – what do you want them to do?

- **Make sure you send them at an appropriate time** – for example, 2am is not appropriate and quickest way to get a cranky message back or bad review.

Of course, lots of businesses, big and small, use SMS to help make our lives easier such as airlines sending reminders, hairdressers and professionals sending appointment reminders and pizza places and supermarkets ensuring we have dinner planned and ready.

Basically, the effectiveness of an SMS campaign depends on various factors, including the relevance of the message, the value it provides to recipients, and the timing of the communication. Always keep the preferences and needs of your target audience in mind when designing your SMS campaigns – that alone will make or break a campaign.

The importance of following up on leads

I have a friend who is a GUN at sales. If you asked me who I thought was the best sales strategist coach, I would say, hands down, Julia Ewert – the Sales Negotiator. The single most important thing Julia has taught me about sales is the money is in the follow-up. According to Julia, the magic (aka the sale) happens around follow-up number seven. But most of us stop following up leads either immediately and most certainly by follow-up number two. It is fair to say that we are ALL leaving money on the table.

Honestly, how many times do you follow up quality leads that come into your business? It's so incredibly easy to keep chasing the next lead, the next sale, the easy sale rather than have a follow-up strategy or process in your business.

How much money do you think you've left on the table, due to the fact that you simply never followed them up? I have to admit, mine would have to be thousands. Following up leads does not come naturally to me, but I am getting better at the process and pushing myself outside my comfort zone to follow things up.

Most of us don't follow up because we are afraid we will be a pest rather than a guest. Or as someone once put it to me, "Be on the way to annoyance-town" or simply a spammer. That would be the worst, right, to be called a spammer? So, what's the trick? There's no trick, but if you always lead with value, think about how you can help them before you think about that money in your bank account, you will 100% be more guest than pest.

Following up on leads – a process to get more sales

- Send a friendly and personalised email within 24-48 hours of initial contact. Thank them for their interest and briefly recap the key points of your conversation.
- If you've had a phone conversation, follow up with a phone call within a few days to check in and see if they need any further assistance.
- Share relevant resources such as blog posts, articles or case studies that align with their needs and interests or solves the problem you are hoping to solve with the product or service you are attempting to sell them. This shows value up front, possibly prompting the idea – if they give this much value for free, imagine what I will get if I do business with them.
- Connect with your leads on social media platforms like LinkedIn or Instagram. Like, comment or share their posts when relevant and

engage with them in a friendly and professional manner. This helps build rapport and keeps you on their radar – brilliant top of mind marketing strategy.

Remember, the key is to strike a balance between staying on their radar, staying top of mind and respecting their boundaries.

Make following up leads a weekly, if not daily, process in your business. Mark your busy diary to follow up leads. If you turn two or even 10 leads a week into a purchase, what would that do for your business over 12 months? This little tip of following up leads could be the marketing strategy, or really sales strategy, that makes your business stronger, better and more profitable.

Ground level marketing – write on the footpath

Yes, it's exactly as it sounds – use the footpath around your business or in your town to market your business. Of course, make sure you don't need any permits from your local council to do so – I don't want to get you into any strife!

My local gym celebrated its fifth birthday doing this and it was quite impressive. On the footpath was a mixture of birthday messaging, gym membership specials and thank-you messages. They wrote on the footpath down our main street, on popular street corners, on the footpath over the bridges – and they were just the ones I saw in my daily walking and shopping life.

Our indigenous group did something similar to celebrate NAIDOC Week a few years back. They drew footprints and wrote messages around the town to bring awareness around NAIDOC Week to everyone going about their daily lives.

It's not a marketing strategy you'd do every day or every week, but when something special is happening in your business, it might be a great way to grab attention outside posting on social media and sending out an email.

Side note: Using environmentally friendly and pet friendly chalk means that it will wash away in the next rain and do no harm.

Art meets branding – commission a mural

Take writing on the footpath to the next level and commission a mural! It's very left of field when it comes to thinking about a marketing strategy but stick with me here. Think about that blank wall either inside or outside your building that no-one notices and creates no return for you whatsoever, because it's just a wall. Then think about people stopping to look and take photos of your amazing commissioned mural wall. A mural that represents your values, your brand and you. Most street artists or muralists enjoy collaborating with their clients, and are also keen to share their works of art in progress on their socials. The process of painting is also quite a crowd-attractor – many local people enjoy watching the painting in progress.

Of course, if you don't own the building you will need to get permission and your local council will also need to be consulted.

Jumbled, in Orange, NSW, commissioned a beautiful mural on the outside wall of their building. It features so much on their social media and people love having their photos taken in front of it and tagging Jumbled. They then post on their own socials – that's known, my friend, as UGC (User Generated Content) and also known as free marketing.

Silo Art is now a whole tourist attraction, especially in Victoria. People can enjoy driving from one mural to the next along the Silo Art Trail, exploring our beautiful regional and rural areas, learning more about the area and spending money in small towns and communities.

It's definitely an out of the box thinking marketing strategy, but if you have a blank wall at your place of business, it could be an exciting one to explore.

Host webinars and share your knowledge

Never underestimate what you know that others would like to know.

Webinars are a great way to share that knowledge online with an audience locally, nationally or even internationally. A webinar, put simply, is a seminar or workshop held over the internet. There are loads of platforms you can use to host a webinar, as simple as Zoom

"

**Never underestimate
what you know that others
would like to know.**

"

or Google Meet for instance. Or you can get more webinar focused platforms such as GoToWebinar, Easy Webinar and WebinarNinja.

Webinars are no different from any other marketing strategy – know why you're doing it and know the outcome you hope to achieve. Webinars are particularly effective for educational and informative content, product demonstrations, expert interviews and industry updates.

Webinars are great in most stages of your customer or client journey. They are great for attracting cold traffic – someone who has never heard of you but your webinar topic sounds interesting to them. And they are great for nurturing warm and hot traffic as well. You can run a webinar just for existing clients or customers, or you can run one to bring in new business.

The benefits of hosting webinars

Why are they so good? They:

- provide an opportunity to establish trust with your audience
- attract individuals who are genuinely interested in your product or service
- are interactive, allowing for direct communication with your audience through chat, polls and Q&A sessions
- overcome time and geographic constraints, especially when made available on-demand. This broadens your potential audience
- can serve as a valuable source of content for your website. By repurposing webinar content into multiple blog posts, shareable pieces and videos, you can generate a substantial amount of new content, providing ongoing value to your audience.

So, what do you know that someone else might like to know that you could turn into a webinar? Think about the questions you are asked all the time by your customers or clients. Think how you could tell more people the answers, while attracting more quality leads and potentially, being paid to share your knowledge. Webinars can be free, if that works best with your overall marketing strategy, but often you do pay to attend.

There are two types of webinars – evergreen and live webinars. Evergreen means that it was originally recorded live but now it is repeated and there is no ability to interact with the host, as it's not live. Live is clearly the opposite – the host is there in real time talking and sharing with you and you are able to ask questions, get answers and interact with others on the webinar.

Live webinars are best when you want real-time interaction, timely content, a sense of urgency or guest speakers. Evergreen webinars are more flexible, scalable, perfectible, and suitable for lead generation and evergreen content. Choose based on your goals, content type and audience preferences. Consider using both formats for different purposes.

Don't be afraid to try new things. And don't be afraid to let technology or your lack of perceived expertise hold you back from amazing marketing strategies such as hosting webinars.

Host workshops for hands-on brand engagement

Presenting a workshop is also a way to share your value and expertise, but is done face to face or IRL as the kids say these days! (IRL = In Real Life.)

This is the most powerful marketing strategy that I have used to grow my marketing strategy business. To date, I have probably hosted around 336 workshops. That's 336-plus times I have stood in front of a live small business audience, big or small, and talked about marketing.

Benefits of hosting a workshop

The reasons you host a workshop are similar to why you host a webinar:

- Workshops provide an opportunity to establish trust with your audience by offering valuable information.
- You can position yourself as a trusted resource, you can nurture relationships with your community, even before they consider making a purchase.
- Workshops attract individuals who are genuinely interested in your product or service.
- Workshops are in real life and are therefore, by their very nature, interactive. People can get a real sense of who you are, what you know and if you are a good fit for them pretty quickly in a workshop situation.

You will need to consider the location, venue size, catering, workbooks, tech required, and non-tech things like whiteboards and computer cables. Omygoodness, if I had a dollar for every time the computer cable was the issue with connectivity, I could probably buy an island. Well okay, maybe not a whole island but I do have a whole range of cords and adapters I don't go to any workshop without!

Just like webinars, workshops are particularly effective for educational and informative content, product demonstrations, expert interviews and industry updates. If your business can provide valuable insights through live presentations, workshops are for you.

Workshops can be for three people or 300 people – depending on the outcome you want for your business and for your customer. Again, as with everything, it is important to ensure you know the goal (reason) for the workshop, what success would look like (the ROI – Return On Investment) and that you market the workshop to the right audience so you get bums on seats.

You are an expert in something – it is that thing you do as a business owner. I know from living in a rural area all my life that communities are crying out for workshops that teach what it is that you do. Small communities are often under-resourced with expertise in many areas, but there is enormous expertise and wisdom in your area. It's just that very few people step up and say, "Hey, want to learn how to set up your own website, cook an Indian feast or encourage a love of reading for your children?" I really want to encourage you to share your knowledge and host workshops or webinars, if it suits your business model and will help attract quality leads and make you more profitable. *Go for it.* This is one of my favourite marketing strategies – workshops. Maybe I could come to your hometown one day and host a workshop as a collaboration with you? Let's chat about that idea some more!

Leveraging suppliers for marketing support

If your business has suppliers of products, whether that be retail products you on-sell through your online store or bricks and mortar store or whether the product is a photocopier from the local copy house, ask yourself how your suppliers could help market your business. This is almost a one-percenter because you already have the suppliers, but perhaps you aren't using them to your marketing advantage.

Enlisting your suppliers for help

You could encourage your suppliers to help you market your business in the following ways:

- Place you as a preferred retailer or a customer on their website with a link back to your website. Quality links are good for SEO, but it makes good business sense to have your name on their website directory.

- As you spend money with them, perhaps they can give a little back and support you with some freebies which you can use in a variety of ways. You could:

  - use them as a prize in a competition. In my retail days, we would ask our suppliers to supply a monthly prize which sat on our counter. We asked customers if they would like to enter into this month's prize draw and we would collect their name, email and address. In exchange, we would mention the supplier on our socials and website and actively promote that they were the sponsor of this month. For us, it was all about data collecting and gathering email addresses for marketing purposes. Yes, of course, we asked their permission as they were filling out the form – we only wanted happy people on our list!

  - use them as a gift to your top clients or customers as a thank-you for doing business with us gift. This would surely surprise and delight your customers.

  - give them to your staff as employee rewards or incentives.

  - use them as free gifts and incentives to customers who participate in a survey you are conducting or leave you a five-star review.

- Tag them in your social posts and send them a little DM (direct message) or email asking them to share the post you have tagged them in, so that the people following them also see your post.

- Find ways you could collaborate with them. Propose joint marketing campaigns or promotions with your suppliers. This can include co-branded advertising, cross-promotion or shared content creation.
- Co-create content with them. Videos, blogs, podcasts, Instagram lives – there are lots of content you could create together and therefore leverage both audiences.
- Explore sponsorship opportunities with your suppliers.

If there's a marketing strategy in this book that you'd like to try, but are not sure you have the resources or expertise to pull it off – would it work if you involved your supplier?

The list of ways your suppliers can help promote your business is vast, very vast. You need to think outside the marketing square to imagine it. Hopefully some of the suggestions here will help inspire thoughts of marketing greatness.

Seizing speaking opportunities

For many people, public speaking is feared more than death according to numerous internet sources, highlighting the fear and anxiety that many people experience when faced with the prospect of public speaking. Perhaps this sounds like you?

It definitely sounded like me until I turned 40. I think I was 41 or 42 when I enrolled in a professional speaking program. I am not one hundred percent sure what made me enrol, but it was a good challenge and a great chance to step outside my comfort zone. And it certainly was that.

Now I love speaking. I love standing in front of an audience and sharing my knowledge, answering their questions and seeing the "aha" moments from the audience, those moments when you go "Aha! Now I get it." Those moments are gold for a speaker like me. No feedback is required if I can see these aha moments during my presentation as I know I have made a difference.

But you don't have to speak for a living to use speaking opportunities to grow your business. In your community right now, I am sure there are groups of people who would love you to come along and share your story, your wisdom or do a "how to" for them. Think Rotary clubs, Probus clubs, chambers, sporting clubs, just to name a few. Your type of business would determine which groups would be ideal for you to get in front of.

Wisdom from speaking at events

If speaking is something you would love to stretch yourself to do, even make money from doing, here are some lessons I've learned or wisdom I'd like to share:

- Just start. I really wanted to put "get a speaking coach" first but you just need to start. If you wait for the right speaking coach, you might never do it. Reach out to your local Rotary club and ask if you can come and share your story with them or google your local Toastmasters group.
- Get a speaking coach or join a course specifically for teaching you how to speak on stage. I still get butterflies before I take the stage, but I no longer vomit before I have to go on (yes, this did happen several times in the early days).
- Stand in front of your camera and practise presenting. No-one ever has to see the footage, but it will tell you so much about the way you present and talk, the good, the bad and the downright sensational bits.
- Start writing down stories. Stories engage an audience, makes your message powerful, memorable and relatable. Comedians are the best at this – stories are just about all they have in the whole routine. Stories are your best friend when public speaking. Tell more stories.
- Just be you. Don't be anyone else.
- Only take feedback from people who are entitled to give feedback. One of my favourite sayings is: *don't let the people in the cheap seats have an expensive opinion.* In other words, unless the person giving

you the feedback (specifically on your public speaking) is a person brave enough to do public speaking themselves, be wary of letting what they say affect what you do next.

You are never too old or too young to develop the public speaking skill. It is a fast way to build trust, create brand awareness and to build a community of buyers and referers of business. Do you think you might be willing to stretch yourself and do some public speaking?

Bridge the digital and physical with QR codes

QR Codes – I have long loved these little pieces of gold. I used them 10 years ago in marketing and had to explain to others how to use them as they didn't really work that well. But now, now everyone knows how to use them, thanks to the pandemic.

How do you make a QR code? My best suggestion is www.canva.com – if you don't have an account already, you can sign up for free and create one. Canva makes QR code building super easy – literally in two or three clicks you can create one and start using it.

Side note: After you make one, make sure you test it yourself before using it – make sure it does actually work!

Using QR codes

Here are a few places where QR codes are gold:

- Whether you have a printed business card to physically hand to people or a digital version, a QR code is an amazing way of making one thing into loads of things! Scan my QR code on my business card and up pops a mobile friendly webpage created especially for meeting new people. There's a welcome, links to social platforms and a website and maybe even a special freebie, specifically designed to surprise and delight new connections.

- Create a survey through Google Forms or Survey Monkey, and use a QR code to link to the survey and get customer feedback.

- Link to exclusive coupons, discounts or even competitions.

- Think about how you could use QR codes in your business to surprise and delight your customer. Maybe it's an exclusive piece of video content for them, your favourite playlist on Spotify (think the old-fashioned mixtapes!), storytelling or giving more information on a product or service. If it's a product, maybe it's suggestions on how else you could use the product, other than its original use. The Facebook group for Kmart products with multiple uses have wonderful creative ideas – for example, multiple ways to use your old candle jars when the candle is finished. Pinterest has a thousand ideas, too. Imagine when someone buys your candle, the QR code sends them to a Pinterest board with loads of ideas of what they can do to recycle the candle when it's done. Customer experience is everything.

- If you have a physical location, create a QR code which links to a virtual tour of your business.

I have to say I do love a restaurant that offers QR code ordering! And I've seen QR codes used well in TV commercials recently. When music is being played on a TV commercial, there's a code to scan to get the music – genius collaboration between brand and artist!

I've also seen them used well on wine bottles. Brown Brothers used them for storytelling but also gave the purchaser an opportunity to tailor the link as part of a gift to someone else. So, someone gets a bottle of wine as a gift, scans the QR code and it's a personalised message from the person who gave it to them! Now that's using tech to create a great experience. JC Penney in the US did something similar with Santa Tags and enabled personalised voice recordings.

CHALLENGE

Embrace the humble QR code in your business and test some examples above. Think outside the square for your own business and experiment with how QR codes can not only create a better customer experience in your business, but also make it simpler.

Entering and leveraging awards

If applying for awards isn't in your marketing strategy, then make it part of your marketing strategy. Seriously, if you want cred in your space, if you want to become the go-to person in your industry or if you simply want to stand out from the crowd – then entering awards is 100% the way to go. Not only do you get leverage, but honestly, most of what you will get from applying for awards can be found in doing the applications, not even winning.

Taking time to look back at what you have achieved, where you have come from to where you are now – that's probably going to give you the most joy. In business we rarely take time to reflect and look back at how far we have come – so if you get nothing else from applying for awards, you will 200% get that.

But let's say you do win or you are a finalist – what now? How can you leverage the heck out of it to help build your business? Get more brand awareness, build creditability, and potentially get more sales.

The benefits of awards

- As a finalist, winner or runner-up, the award host will probably send you a logo or a tile or image to use. This is your licence to add that to just about everywhere you can think of – for example, your LinkedIn profile, on Facebook, in the about section of your Instagram bio and add it to your website and email signature.

- Where can you leverage the words "award-winning" or if you won more than one – "multi-award-winning" business?

- Think about the directories your business is listed in – go and change those.

- Make a bio photo in Canva with the words "award winner" or put the name of the award you won under your bio photo.

- When posting about your win on social media, don't forget to tag and congratulate the other winners, finalists and people in your category. Not only is it good to be humble, but it's good for brand awareness to be tagging other businesses (okay, that's not exactly humble, but it's business and we want the most out of this win).

- If the award hosts didn't supply you with a press release – then write one yourself! Getting your win into the media is a fabulous idea and shouldn't be too hard.

- Write a blog for your website about your win. Use parts of your award-winning application to construct a blog about your business, the ups, the downs, the highs, the lows and share it with your community. Pro tip: Before you send in an award application, make sure you keep a copy for yourself.

- Write an email to your list telling them the good news and thanking them for supporting your now award-winning business!

- Go live on Facebook, Instagram, LinkedIn, whichever platform you perform best on or do them all. Share your win and say thank you to your community.

- Use this award-winning application to apply for more awards.

- Use the win as a fabulous excuse to pitch yourself for podcast interviews, guest blogs and articles.

You don't need to do all this straightaway – although lots of it you should – you can milk this win/finalist thing for months and even in 12 months use it as a "remember when".

Awards have creditability. Awards have a long shelf life – so your win should have a long shelf life too. Oh and again, if entering awards isn't on your marketing strategy list – then it's time it was.

CHALLENGE

Research what awards you have locally and even nationally that you could apply for. Take note on their opening dates and put them into the calendar for future reference. Get curious and get yourself the credibility you deserve. As a country business owner, you are eligible for the Australian Rural Business Awards that open in the early part of the year – so watch for those awards, if no other.

The prestige of judging awards

Have you ever considered judging an awards program as part of your marketing strategy? I have judged several awards including local ones for a local Chamber of Commerce, online marketing ones and even some international business awards.

The advantages of judging awards

There are many business advantages to being a judge of an awards program, especially if it is your field of expertise or wheelhouse.

- Credibility and authority – being recognised as an expert in your field will build know, like and trust within your community.

- Visibility and exposure are another obvious advantage. Your name, photo and expertise will be featured on event websites, promotional materials and media coverage, exposing you to a broader audience.

- Networking opportunities in abundance (hopefully). You'll interact with other experts, influential figures and key players in your industry, leading to potential collaborations, partnerships or invitations to other industry events.

- Having your brand associated with prestigious awards or well-known organisations can positively impact your personal brand or business.

- A position of thought leadership because as a judge, you'll likely have the chance to share your insights and expertise through interviews, panel discussions or articles. This helps establish you as a thought leader, further boosting your reputation and brand awareness.

- Increased online presence due to the media coverage and social media coverage of the awards. Most awards can't happen without judges.

- Helps you stand out from your competitors. Being chosen as a judge sets you apart from competitors who may not have similar accolades. This unique distinction can give you a competitive advantage and help you stand out in a crowded marketplace.

And then there's some long-term benefits in the recognition and connections you make during the awards event but hopefully well into the future, too.

Sometimes we do these things, like being judges for events and award programs, but perhaps we don't think of them as a marketing strategy or as a business activity that can help us as much as it helps the organisation running the awards. It's time to think a little differently.

Subscription boxes for curated brand experiences

Subscription boxes are on the rise here in Australia, so you might be seeing more and more subscription boxes popping up as people's businesses. In the US they are wildly popular. (They are something I hope to do one day, to have a subscription box business model but that's a tale for another day.)

So what is a subscription box? A subscription box is a recurring delivery of curated products or services that customers receive on a regular basis like monthly or quarterly. Each box typically contains a variety of items related to a specific theme or niche. Subscription boxes can range from beauty and fashion products to gourmet food, books, fitness gear and more. Hometastic run by the amazing Jane, one of my clients, has a subscription box for homewares she sends out quarterly. Michelle Smith has Aussie Biz Chic, which is a subscription box for office/business products. There's also Renae from Boxed in the Bush and how could I forget Liz, from the Australian Cake Decorators Network, who posts out hundreds of pink boxes each month with cake decorating items for all her subscribers? These are just a few examples of subscription box businesses in my world.

So, how can you use subscription boxes to market your business? Well, you could create one but that's a whole other business model or you can market your products or services through these boxes. Most people who have a subscription box business are always on the hunt for amazing products to put in their boxes or if you are a serviced-based business, you could approach them to put a flyer or brochure in their boxes for a fee. This could be a great way to reach new audiences and increase brand visibility or make more sales if they are prepared to buy 100 products from you to put in their subscription boxes. You might need to negotiate some terms to get your products or service brochures into the box but it's a great way to introduce yourself to their subscriber base and introduce your products and services to a new audience. This could be a one-off transaction or could lead to a long-standing collaboration – who knows?

Often subscription boxes have themes such as Christmas, and other holiday and seasonal releases. So how could that work with your business? And if you do get your products or services into their boxes, what could you offer them in return? Perhaps it's more of a partnership deal where they put your product or flyer in their box and you offer them the opportunity to market to your customers, your list, on your socials to help build their audience too. Really, anything is possible.

By strategically leveraging subscription boxes, you can broaden your reach and achieve increased brand awareness and recognition and of course, this all needs to lead to more sales. What do you think? A good "out of the box" marketing strategy? Who knows, you might have even got a copy of this book through a subscription box?

Engage your community with a challenge or quiz

People love a good challenge or quiz as they appeal to a person's innate desire for interaction and validation. Challenges are also a great marketing strategy, especially for list building. They're not so great for direct sales, but excellent for getting people onto your email list. These engaging tools not only capture attention but also foster brand awareness, engagement and customer loyalty.

Quizzes and challenges can take many forms and can be easy or complex. My 5 Day Social Media Challenge (https://bit.ly/5daysocialchallenge) is done via email, with an email drip fed each day into the subscriber's inbox. You could use a platform like TryInteract (https://www.tryinteract.com/) that has tonnes of quiz creation templates to help you set up your quiz super easily.

For quizzes think "Which Disney princess are you?" or "What does your dream kitchen looks like?" or "What's your core purpose?" or "What type of business owner are you?" Omygoodness, the ideas and capabilities are endless. But of course, it all needs to come back to business – *for what purpose?* What's the goal? How are you going to market it and what are you going to do with the results? No use going 110% in on creating a challenge or a quiz and having tonnes of new people in your world if you don't have a plan on what's next for them.

Quizzes and challenges can breathe life into your marketing strategy by turning passive consumers into active participants. These interactive tools boost engagement, gather valuable data and create a memorable experience that lingers in your audience's minds. Embrace the opportunity to connect with your audience on a deeper level and create some dynamic marketing in a marketing world that sometimes seems so beige. Is this something you would use to grow your list and engage your community some more? I think it would be fabulous, if done right.

Creating viral potential with a hashtag (#) campaign

A hashtag campaign can be a fun and engaging marketing strategy. It involves creating a unique hashtag and encouraging your audience to use it when sharing their content related to your business or a specific theme. Think perhaps about a VIP party that you might have or a business birthday celebration. One of the things you could do as part of your marketing is create a unique hashtag for the event that people can use, and therefore you can keep all that content together and also make it more searchable for you and your community.

Obviously, you need to have a goal around what you want to achieve with the hashtag campaign. Is it to increase brand visibility, generate user-generated content, drive sales or foster community engagement? Your goals will shape the campaign's strategy. You'll need to do some research to make sure that the hashtag isn't already widely used and that it doesn't have content based around something that doesn't align with your business values and therefore could be damaging to you and your business.

The success of a hashtag campaign hinges on the promotion of it so that everyone knows to use it. Spread the word about your campaign through your social media profiles, email newsletters, website, tickets to the event if appropriate and other marketing channels. Clearly explain the purpose of the campaign, the hashtag to be used, and any rewards or incentives.

Monitor the campaign hashtag regularly and engage with users who are participating. Like, comment and share their posts to show appreciation for their involvement and 100% encourage participants to create content related to your campaign theme using the hashtag. It could be photos, videos, testimonials, stories, or creative interpretations of your products or services.

And, of course, at the end show gratitude to participants, share a recap of the campaign's highlights, showcase the content created and announce winners if applicable.

Hashtag campaign steps

Let's say you run a small health food store. You want to encourage your customers to adopt healthy eating habits.

Campaign theme: Encouraging customers to share their healthy eating habits and creative recipes.

Hashtag: #HealthyHabitsChallenge

Steps:

- Create promotional graphics announcing the campaign and explaining the rules.
- Share the campaign details on your social media profiles, website and in-store.
- Encourage customers to share photos or videos of their healthy meals using the hashtag #HealthyHabitsChallenge.

- Share participant content on your social media and website, crediting them.
- Offer a discount to participants on their next purchase and a chance to win a gift basket of healthy products.
- Engage with participant posts by liking, commenting and sharing.
- At the end of the campaign, showcase the most creative and inspiring posts, announce the winners and thank everyone for their participation.

Remember that a successful hashtag campaign involves creativity, interaction and providing value to your audience. By doing so, you can strengthen your brand's online presence and build a community around your business.

Pretty cool, hey? A different way to creating community and participation for your business and in your marketing strategy. Have you seen some great ones getting around in the past? Perhaps you should try something like this when you next have a big event or launch coming up.

***

This chapter has been all about thinking outside the box when it comes to your marketing and I hope that I have inspired some thinking or strategising as you've read the different ideas.

Thinking outside the box when it comes to your business and your marketing can be zigging when everyone else is zagging and it can be being brave enough to try something new. As I mentioned at the start, sometimes it's better to create your own path and other times it's better to ride the wave of the latest trend. Knowing when to do what is what sets you apart from your competitors.

Again, if you are stuck in a hole, reached your glass ceiling or just need a marketing challenge, try thinking outside the marketing box.

Chapter 6

HARDER THINGS TO DO

These ideas aren't for everyone but probably should be

I never lose.
I either win or learn.
Each day I win or learn
something new.

——

**Michelle Clark, Judds,
Yarrawonga, Victoria**

There's marketing that is easy to do and just about everyone does it, for example, posting on Facebook. And then there is marketing that is a little harder to do, a little more time consuming and requires more effort, energy and sometimes money. These are the marketing ideas in this chapter. But don't let the idea that they are harder to do put you off them. These ideas are some of the marketing activities that have made a business stand out from the crowd, made a business more profitable and made a business more successful.

Remember, nothing changes if nothing changes. So if you are stuck in marketing la la land and are doing the same marketing activities over and over again, month on month, year on year and wondering why your business isn't growing as fast as it should, then this could be the chapter of the book that moves the needle in your business or at the very least, makes you think differently, more strategically and more holistically about your marketing efforts and strategy.

Getting found on Google with SEO (Search Engine Optimisation)

It's time to talk SEO (Search Engine Optimisation) and web optimisation, those nifty little tools that can put your small business on the digital Google map.

SEO stands for Search Engine Optimisation and it's really about making your website shine like a star in the vast galaxy of the internet. You know those times when you Google something and a bunch of results pop up? SEO helps your website show up in those results, so when someone searches for what you offer and what you sell, they find you with ease – or at least that's the goal.

So why does SEO matter? Because when someone searches keywords or key phrases on what it is that you sell, you want them to see you and your brand. The best way to achieve those eyeballs is being on the first page of search results, like you're the fancy store on Main Street that everyone notices first.

Kate Toon, an extraordinary Australian SEO expert, says that for most people over half of all traffic comes from organic search, (53%: The percentage of all trackable website traffic that comes from organic search – BrightEdge.) Flip that over, and what it means is that ALL OTHER marketing is worth less than half of your traffic. The truth is that traffic from SEO is much more conversion focused as these are active customers, not casual browsers. So the 53% you're getting from organic will likely have a much higher conversion rate than those from socials.

So most of us give no thoughts to showing up on Google through searches of our ideal client or customer, much to our own detriment, as Kate explains.

So it is SEO or social media or both?

Actually, they are the perfect duo. Now, don't get me wrong – social media is fantastic. It's like hosting a party where everyone gets to know you and your business. But here's the thing: social media is the party, and SEO is like making sure your house (your website) is all spruced up and inviting so people want to drop by after the party. Social media has party vibes – you share something and people see it right away (potentially). You chat with customers, show behind-the-scenes stuff and create a vibrant community. Social media is where your brand personality shines – think of it as your fun side.

But SEO is your strong foundation in business. SEO isn't a sprint; it's a marathon. It keeps bringing folks to your website even when the party's over. People actively looking for what you offer will find you, even if they've never heard of your business. Being on the first page of Google means you're trusted and relevant in your field.

> **BONUS TIP**
> Use free tools like Google Analytics and Google Search Console to understand how your website is doing and what keywords people are using to find you.

So, invest some time into your SEO, just like you are constantly investing in social media. Invest some time into SEO activities on your website:

- Look at your website pages' H1 and H2 tag. Your H1 tag is like the headline in a newspaper and it tells Google and your visitors what the page is all about. Take a look in the backend of your website at your H1 tags for a start. H2 and H3 tags are like subheadings – not as important but worth looking at.
- Check to see if the images used on your website had image alt text. Google is pretty smart but not smart enough to know exactly what the photo you've used is all about – so have you labelled it clearly? This isn't just for Google, but also for visually impaired users so their software can tell them what they are looking for.
- Google also likes both internal and external links. Do you have content and pages linking to other pages and other content on your website? For example, check out this blog which then talks about reading another blog from the website. And external links are linking out to other quality websites. Perhaps you've been on a podcast, written an article or won an award, so make sure you link back to their website.

SEO is a huge topic and these three tips above are just the tip of the iceberg. If you want to learn more, head to YouTube and watch some videos, listen to episode 39 of my Small Business Made Simple Podcast with Kate Toon, and join Kate's communities online.

SEO is like your website's secret ingredient, helping it rise to the top of the digital galaxy. Social media and SEO together create a balanced online presence for your business. They both need energy, time and investment.

Side note: No matter how good your SEO is or isn't, a slow loading website will see 61% of people leaving in 5 seconds anyway – so check your website's loading speed before you do too much else! (Use Google loading speed to test.)

CHALLENGE

Earmark some time in your diary to check out how your website is preforming now and seek out some expert help if it needs improving. Make SEO a part of your marketing, just like social media is.

Crafting an effective media press release

If you ever had trouble thinking about what to post on your social media, then spare a thought for all the media organisations in the world who must create new, engaging content for our modern day 24-hour news cycle. The pressure for new content, all the time, would be enormous. So if you think that creating a press release to send into the media about your business, your new product, your point of difference isn't worth it because you're just a small country business, then think again. There's every chance the media will gobble it up because it's new, refreshing and something their readers will engage with.

Rules for writing a press release

- The press release must be newsworthy. This is definitely not an opportunity to write a 400-word blog post on how good you are, how long you have been doing business for and why people should shop with you.

- Unless you are writing for a medical journal, your press release should be clear, concise and simple. Avoid jargon and technical terms only you understand – acronyms are the worst in press releases.

- Have an attention-grabbing headline, and the first paragraph should summarise the key messages in the press release. These two things will ensure the journalist or editor wants to read further.

- Your press release should be accompanied by some high-quality photos that relate to the press release. I highly recommend that at least one of these photos is of you.

- Make sure the release date is noted.

- Make sure you do include your logo, contact details and a short bio, so the journalist can get in touch if they want more information or to send you something – like the link to the published press release.

I love getting media for my businesses. Having media helps with increased visibility for your business, credibility around your content and business reputation, gives you an edge over your competition and helps differentiate yourself from others in the same market.

I've written press releases before that have not only been published in several publications but have resulted in TV and radio interviews and ongoing requests for content. If your press release is media worthy, you'll find it has a longer shelf life than just being published once for one newspaper or magazine.

Here's a sample press release:

Location and date	*Hamilton, New Zealand – November 12, 2023*
Release date	FOR IMMEDIATE RELEASE
Headline	**Competition is Healthy Says Lemonade Stand Queen**
Opening line	Increased competition in the local lemonade stand market should be welcomed, according to the operator of popular lemonade stand 'Shelly's Pure Lemonade'.
	12-year-old Shelly Smith has been selling her home-made brand of lemonade from the footpath in front of her parents' North Street home for 18 months and has seen the highs and lows of the trade.
The 5 Ws & 1 H: **Who, What, Where, When, How and Why**	"Stands come and go", says Ms Smith, "but when there are more stands around the vendors are more serious. They try harder to make a better product. That gives our customers confidence and sales go up."
	In recent months the number of lemonade stands in North Street has risen from three to five. Experts believe this trend will continue, with the possibility of two or even three new stands before the end of summer.
	Ms Smith feels that a stable supply of lemonade will also benefit the street's economy.
	"People know that if they are thirsty, North Street is the place to come. With plenty of lemonade stands on this street it doesn't matter if some of the vendors take a day off. The customer is never disappointed so they always come back."
About you/bio	Shelly Smith is a sole trader of lemonade and occasional cookies. Her stand at 223 North Street is usually open weekdays after school and on weekends, except when she is playing with her friends or watching a movie.
Contact details/ call to action	Contact: Shelly Smith email@example.com 223 North Street Hamilton, New Zealand Ph +64 877 9233
Tell the reader you're finished	END ###

Writing a press release can seem like a big job but I would encourage you to give it a go. Or get a content writer or copywriter to do a draft for you. As with all marketing, know your ideal client and know what return on investment you are expecting and weigh it all up. Stretch yourself and get writing.

Share knowledge and build your brand with blogging

Writing blogs is similar to writing a press release and in fact, once your press release is published, you can republish it on your website as a blog post. Repurposing is my jam. Make sure you read Tip #28.

Blogging originally involved "personal web logs" from which the term "blog" was born. It was more of a personal journal than a marketing tool. But, as with most internet innovations, us small business owners soon saw the marketing potential of having a blog, and it all took off from there.

I write blog posts – weekly. You can find them all at www. socialmediaandmarketing.com.au/blog and although blogging weekly seems like a lot – I'll let you in a little secret – it's all repurposed content. Again, read Tip #28.

Why should you write blog posts?

- Blog posts are social and allow for reader interaction and engagement. Blog posts are great through social media as it gives the reader the ability to comment and have discussions with either the author or fellow readers.
- Search engines LOVE new content, and as a result, writing blogs is a great search engine optimisation (SEO) tool.
- Blogging provides an easy way to keep your customers and clients up-to-date on what's going on, provide tips and tricks and provide great FREE value.
- A blog allows you to build trust and rapport with your prospects and show your EXPERTISE in your field.

However, there are some downsides to blogging too. Not the least of which is TIME. Blogging takes a lot of time. For writing blogs to be effective at SEO and engaging readers, they need to be updated regularly. The success from writing blogs comes from having people return, time and time again, to read what's new. This means generating content at least weekly, and that takes time.

Of course, blogging weekly means creating lots of content, constantly coming up with topics and ideas to write about. Have you ever thought about starting a blog? Check out my How to Start a Blog – 22-Point Checklist – scan the QR code at the back of the book for this invaluable resource.

Once you have a blog up and going, don't forget to share it on social platforms and share it more than once. If only between 2-5% of your audience see your posts on socials organically, then repurposing your blog posts at a different time, on a different day, is almost certain to be seen by a different audience.

Only about 1% of internet users produce content online – the remaining 99%? They just consume. By blogging, you stand out from the pack of content consumers, show your expertise and connect with people who you might never have come across otherwise. Those relationships can prove to be invaluable to your business.

Expand your reach with guest blogging

If you don't want to start your own blog, if blogging consistently isn't your thing, then consider writing a blog for someone else – be a guest blogger.

The benefits of guest blogging

The many benefits of guest blogging include:

- increase reach for your content, brand and business
- increase credibility and establish your expertise online
- freshen your content strategy
- increase your site's ranking in search engine searches

- boost traffic and SEO to your website
- drive more sales and qualified leads
- win-win partnerships with another business owner
- improve writing and other content marketing skills
- you get a link back from their website to yours to share on your socials and through other marketing channels.

Of course, you only want to guest blog for other businesses that align with your values, have your ideal client as their audience and are prepared to share your content with their audience. Topic ideas can be the same as those I suggested earlier for blogging, you just need to ensure that guest blogging will help you achieve your own business goals.

Guest blogging is a great way to dip your toe into the water if you aren't a confident writer or you are new at writing for your business.

BONUS TIP

Everyone starts with one blog post. No-one is an expert blogger having only written one or no blogs, so start. Just start. Or hire a content writer or copywriter to help you create a blog or a series of blog posts to send as guest blogs.

Guest blog opportunities

- Look for blogs that are related to your industry or niche, using search engines like Google or Bing. Use keywords related to your niche and add "write for us" or "guest post" to your search to find blogs that accept guest posts.
- Use social media – follow other bloggers or content writers in your niche on social media platforms like Twitter, Facebook and LinkedIn. They may share guest blogging opportunities or have their own blogs that accept guest posts.
- Research your competitors' backlinks – look at the backlinks of your competitors' websites to see if they have any guest posts on other blogs. This can help you identify potential guest blogging opportunities.

- Industry Associations and Chambers of Commerce – look for industry associations and chambers of commerce in your niche or location. These organisations often have blogs and may accept guest posts from members or partners. This can be a great way to get exposure within your industry or local community.

Remember to always check the blog's guest posting guidelines and follow them closely. If you're super keen on doing some guest blogging and what you have to say will help small business owners like us, then reach out. I am always looking for guest bloggers. Check out my blog and guest blogger blogs on my website at www.socialmediaandmarketing.com.au/blog.

> **CHALLENGE**
>
> Write a blog. Just start. Go to Google, ChatGPT, or Facebook Groups, find questions your ideal client is asking and write a blog answering that question. Upload it to your website and share on your socials. Remember, never underestimate what you know that others would like to know. You can do this.

Targeted exposure with in-blog marketing

Rather than writing blog posts or guest blogging, another blogging opportunity or marketing opportunity can be found in advertising on someone's blog. This could be either on their actual blog page on their website or within their blogs. Remember that the title of this chapter is 'Harder things to do' and advertising on a blog isn't a common marketing strategy employed by many. But if you get it right, if you advertise on the right blog, the leads will be quality and you can produce good sales from an audience that might not have known you existed except from the ad you have placed in this blog.

How do you go about doing this? Take notice of blogs you read that have ads in them or on the website you are directed to, or simply reach out to bloggers you follow, admire or know and ask! Asking is the best way to get most things and get most information in business.

Use your voice to grow your brand – host a podcast

When it comes to podcasting, I am completely biased. Podcasting is something I love. I started my Small Business Made Simple Podcast in December 2018 and at the time of writing this book, I am still producing weekly podcasts. Podcasting has done more for my business, brand awareness, sales and for my reputation as a small business, marketing and social media expert than any other marketing activity in my business, ever. So, again, I am just a wee bit biased. I have also produced two seasonal podcasts – *Stories From the Bush* and *Along the Murray*.

Over the next three tips I am going to explain why starting a podcast, sponsoring a podcast and/or being a guest on a podcast is a marketing activity you should consider, no matter where you are in your business – 10 years or longer in or 10 minutes in. Again, this chapter is all about stretching your thinking and stretching your comfort zone into marketing activities that aren't the norm.

If you don't listen to podcasts – then start. Start with mine – Small Business Made Simple, available on most podcast apps, or of course, on my website, www.socialmediaandmarketing.com.au/podcast.

Podcasting is a great way to build an audience, build trust with that audience, become the expert in your field and the go-to person. It's a great way to meet new people (as guests on your show) and for forming friendships and relationships with other people in your industry.

The reason I started a podcast was because I'd just left a marketing business in which I was the integral social media marketer, the COO and the CMO. The end of that partnership was swift and necessary. But it did leave me without a business. I hadn't grown my brand within that business, which was a big mistake, so now I found myself thinking, *there's literally one of me for every corner, of every street, in Australia.* How was I going to stand out from the crowded marketplace? The answer was, of course, podcasting.

This is how could I grow my brand, share my expertise, get new clients, become the go-to person and give exceptional value.

So, I literally went to YouTube and typed in "How to Start a Podcast", because I had no idea where to start.

Next, I wrote down a list of all the things I thought I could talk about and all the people I thought I could reach out to and ask to be a guest on my podcast. I brainstormed 27 episode ideas, including guest names, and thought 27 seemed like a good number and I'd just give it a go. I am very much a Ready, Fire, Aim person (as discussed in Tip #1), so I just started. Clearly, I had a lot more to say than 27 episodes worth of material because now I'm in the hundreds. That list of people I know has grown too because I have had over 100-plus amazing guests on my podcast, all of whom I now have a unique relationship with.

What I learned very early on in my podcasting journey is that people rarely say no to being asked if they'd like a guest spot on a podcast. Of everyone I have asked, only two people have ever said no. They weren't really a no, it was more the case that they said "not now, maybe later in the year." So, that's extraordinary. But when your podcast is in the top 1.5% of international podcasts, according to Listen Notes, you don't have to ask many guests to come in, and in fact people are itching to be a guest and they reach out to you.

So, who should start a podcast? Anyone! Simply, anyone! But just like any business or marketing strategy, you do have to have a strategy behind it.

- Does your audience listen to podcasts?
- Who is the ideal audience for yours?
- What would the overall theme of the podcast be? For example, mine is called, and has the overall theme of, "Small Business Made Simple".
- Do I have time to be consistent with a podcast?
- What's the outcome I am looking for?

Start with the end in mind. Know the goal of the podcast – to entertain, to teach, for brand awareness, to share my expertise, to help small business owners grow their business – you choose, just know the end goal.

Podcast checklist

- A name for the podcast – check to see if it's already taken, register any domains and social handles needed. When naming, think keywords for searchability – because unless you're already famous, people might not find you by your name or some quirky play on words – simple and direct is best. Small Business Made Simple – if you read the title, you pretty much know what the podcast is about! Side Note: I kind of buggered up my name at first. I called my podcast the "Small Business Made Simple Podcast" – I had the word podcast on the end. This opened up the door for someone else to take the name "Small Business Made Simple" – which gutted me. But this someone was an American male, so I didn't think anyone would get us mixed up and by the time I was about 150 episodes in, he had changed his podcast name. It worked out in the end, but it did cause me a lot of stress in the early days. So be careful when claiming your podcast name.

- The format of the podcast – solo episodes, interview style, or both, repurposing your YouTube Channel or Instagram Lives.
- Length of show – in particular, think about your audience. My audience is made up of busy small business owners, so I like to stick to below 20 minutes – however the interviews often go over, because my guests are just fabulous! But I think 20 minutes of listening to just me is enough!
- Equipment – see the PDF guide for a list of equipment I use via the QR code at the back of the book.
- Artwork – you'll need a podcast cover image.

If you're keen to start podcasting, I have included a link to my Podcasting Workbook at the back – scan that QR code to get the workbook. Download it and work through it to help you get started.

Share your expertise and be a guest on a podcast

Regardless of whether you have your own podcast or not, another marketing strategy you could implement is being a guest on a podcast and sharing your knowledge and expertise with someone else's audience.

Pitching to go on someone's podcast is like pitching for anything really when you want to get in front of someone's audience. But – let's start with what NOT to do.

Just like marketing isn't about you (sorry if you thought it was), pitching isn't about you either. It's always customer centric, it's always about what you can do for their audience. When you are pitching, keep this front and centre of your mind. If you write a pitch, just as if you write copy for your website, don't write – I do this and I have done that, I can and I can't … It's NOT customer centric – it's about you.

As a podcast host myself, it takes an enormously huge amount of energy and effort to build an audience who will listen to your podcast week after week, episode after episode. You are building a fan base, a community, and that takes work. So, the people you let in the ears of your treasured audience need to be vetted and need be a good fit for the podcast. I need them to be experts in their field.

So how do you pitch yourself?

Pitching yourself

- Make the pitch conversational. Take the time to listen to some of their podcasts (trust me, we get enough pitches to know when you are lying and haven't really listened to any). Do your research – be social on social with them first.

- Tell the podcast owner/host what you would like to talk to their audience about. Give your chat a title and list three or four things under that topic you think their audience would get value from. Pitch an outcome for their audience.

- Make your pitch short and sharp.

- In order to make the pitch/email short and sharp, have a one pager. This one pager has your details on it, a list of proposed topics, a few short paragraphs about who you are and perhaps even some other media highlights – like "I've been featured on X, Y and Z podcasts" and include logos of where else you've been featured. As much as the pitch isn't about you, the podcast host still wants to get to know you a little and make sure you are qualified to talk about the amazing topic you have pitched. I have a one pager – if you are interested, email me at jenn@jenndonovan.com.au and I will send you a copy to use as a template.

- Make your pitch unique and know who you are pitching to. No use pitching as a YouTube expert to a podcast host who's just had two YouTube experts on the podcast in the past few months.

Maybe you're wondering – well that's all good information, Jenn, but why would I want to go on someone else's podcast as a guest? What's in it for me? LOADS, just loads. A few great reasons are:

- setting yourself up as the expert in your field
- getting in front of a new audience who doesn't know who you are or what you can do for them
- stepping outside your comfort zone
- creating some great content you can repurpose – YAY for that
- creating a new connection and extending your network through conversation
- expanding your brand awareness
- developing your speaking skills
- and, although not the entire purpose or reason, you can potentially make some more sales.

CHALLENGE

Pitch yourself for a podcast. Do some research on who has a podcast that would have the same audience as you, get my one pager, create your own, do up a pitch email to them, highlighting what you can give to their audience and ask if they are looking for new guests. The worst that can happen is that you learn something and they say no, not at the moment.

BONUS TIP

Even if podcast guesting isn't your thing right now, these little pieces of advice work well also to pitch a blog for someone's audience or to pitch to go on someone's YouTube Channel or TV network – any occasion when you are pitching your expertise to get in front of another person's audience.

Associative branding – sponsoring a podcast

Still on podcasting #sorrynotsorry – have you ever thought to sponsor a podcast episode or series? Admittedly though, not every podcast offers adverts. I have offered them on and off over the years. It would be a matter of doing some research (that is, listening to their podcast) to find out who does and who does not offer advertising on their podcasts.

Of course, there are podcasts like those that are under the Mamamia brand that all have advertising. The advertising is part of their revenue streams and the business is podcasting – as opposed to my business where podcasting is a lead generator and community builder.

When thinking about sponsoring a podcast, first consider their audience, their listeners – are they your audience, your buyers? The next important thing to think about is the "call-to-action" that you will use in the advert. If someone is listening to the podcast and hears your advert, what action do you want them to take? How likely are they to take it and how much effort will it take for them to take that action? For example, a call-to-action such as Follow Us on Facebook is too low impact. Very few listeners will take the action of getting out of their podcast app, going into Facebook, searching your business name and clicking like. And if they do, whoopi-do really, you have another like – now what?

You really have to think about what you want someone to do and how easy it will be to do and how powerful the call-to-action is. Humans are very lazy, you know, and because it's a podcast, there's no link to click. They are listening, not reading. And often listening while driving or walking or at the gym, so they're not really able to stop and undertake your call to action.

Other key things to keep in mind, consider and ask the host about before sponsoring a podcast would be:

- know the audience
- check out the content
- look at pricing and packages
- make sure you ask the host about their schedule and availability

- have fun with creative advert
- ask the host about the metrics and reporting they provide.

Prices for sponsoring a single podcast episode can range from as little as $50 to as much as $30K-plus, depending on what podcast you want to sponsor. Yes, I did say $30,000.

Exclusive engagement with a VIP membership

I talk a lot about building community and thinking about your audience more like a community than, well, an audience. A community of followers, people, likers, to know, like and trust you will always grow your business faster than an audience will. So having that ability to *put a picket fence* around your community and nurture them until they are ready to buy or buy again, makes perfect sense.

One marketing strategy for this is to start a membership group or a VIP group. It can be either paid or unpaid, but membership does lend itself to being a paid option rather than a free option.

The easiest example to give you regarding a VIP group is a Facebook group. Regardless of whether it's a paid or free option, the reason for it is the same from a marketing point of view. Build trust quicker, provide content that's not really provided by you elsewhere, give your community a better, more personal experience and the ultimate goal is to make the sales process of community member to buyer, run more smoothly and more quickly. Instead of 10, 15 or 20 touchpoints before you make the sale, it's two or three touchpoints, because they are already so heavily invested in you from being a part of your VIP or membership group.

The benefits of a membership or VIP group

- Marketing strategies such as just posting on our Facebook Pages is no longer allowing us to engage with our audience. Reach is at an all-time low – somewhere between, statistically, 1-5% of our "likers" actually see our posts.

- As mentioned earlier, you can build a fence around your people. It's part of our human makeup that we all want somewhere to belong.
- It's about the community and not always about you. Building a community online with a VIP membership or group brings people with a common goal together – that goal might be you and your business, but it is what everyone has in common.

A membership or a VIP group might be a great marketing strategy for you if:

- You are finding it hard to get any good traction or organic reach with your other marketing strategies, such as posting on social media.
- You're tired of wasting your time with your marketing, especially social media, because it's just not getting the return on investment that you need or making the sales that you want. You are future proofing your business.
- Want to build a community of people – a place where your tribe can give support to each other, a place where your ideal audience can learn, grow and share their journeys?
- You think you have value to offer – if you could just get in front of the right people, you could help them, inspire them and give enormous value?
- You want to get to know your audience more intimately – the better we know and understand them, the better your marketing strategies can be.
- Or maybe if you answer NO to this question – is there a group serving your people, your ideal audience, already in a value adding, inspiring way (how you would do it) – then maybe that's all you need to know to start your membership or group.

Oh, and just in case you're wondering when the perfect time to start your VIP membership or group is – IT'S NOW!

I can't finish this tip without inviting you into the community I'm building – my Facebook Group, Like Minded Business Owners – I would absolutely love to see you in there. Make sure when you join, you say hi and tell me you've arrived since reading my book.

Reframe the use of influencers in your business

Influencer marketing is something we see on our social feeds every day. Some celebrity telling us to use this product because they supposedly do. Depending on your relationship with that influencer, you may or may not buy what they are marketing and may or may not scroll past it.

Influencers have influence. They have built "trust" (I use that term loosely when I talk about celebrity influencers, because can you really build trust with someone who just wants to sell you something over and over again?) with their audience. Their audience trusts when they say they used something, had a great experience or purchased something, so their audience is more likely to purchase said product, experience or thing.

Having someone else tell your audience just how amazing you are, or how amazing your product is, is worth its weight in gold if done right. Having someone else help build that know, like, (or love) and trust factors is almost priceless.

We need to stop thinking about influencer marketing as paying a celebrity to show your product, and start thinking of influencers as the customer who tagged you on Instagram when they took a photo of your product and shared it with their audience.

Think of influencers as your amazing staff member who always shares your stuff on their socials or to their friends, or that customer who is always referring you new business. Here's a fact – 92 percent of people trust other consumer recommendations over business advertising. These people, therefore, are your influencers. Not the celebrities but the customers you have now, the staff, family and friends who already support you, the people who refer business to you over and over again – these are the people you need to think of as your influencers. And how many of those do you have? How big is that opportunity?

How can you encourage your staff, family and friends to share your content with their family and their friends, using their influence, to get more brand awareness for your business and create, hopefully, more

"

We need to stop thinking about influencer marketing as paying a celebrity to show your product, and start thinking of influencers as the customer who tagged you on Instagram when they took a photo of your product and shared it with their audience.

"

sales? This is influencer marketing for us. Your community probably already supports your business (it's the country way), but how can you make it more strategic rather than random and done out of the goodness of their heart?

A small retail business in western Queensland harnessed this process in a very strategic way. They had a system where you could apply to be an affiliate with them but their affiliates were really influencers. Their program looked like this –

- Join as an affiliate and buy their products at 30% off (some exclusions applied).
- Promote the products you purchased – that's why there's 30% off as a reward.
- Offer your followers, your community, a coupon for 15% off any products they buy from the store – this is the bit I loved.

Clearly this business had a good markup – being able to offer 45% off most products. But just as clearly, they knew the power of other people promoting their products and to them the discount wasn't just a discount, but a marketing expense. Some businesses pay for Google or social media ads – they offered affiliate or influencer deals as their marketing spend.

Think about influencers not just as famous people on Instagram, but as the people in your community who already buy from you, who already know, like and trust you. Reward them somehow so they can be your "micro influencers" as I like to call them.

Reward referrals with an affiliate program

Do you have something you sell like a course or program, a service or even a product? Would having other people marketing your product or service help you make more sales? Do you have a markup on your product or service that you could sacrifice to make more sales?

If you answered yes to these questions, then having an affiliate program might be something you could implement in your business. Affiliate programs work best for businesses that offer products or services that are in demand and have a broad appeal. If you have a niche product or service, an affiliate program may not be the best fit.

Affiliate programs typically offer a percentage of the sale as commission to affiliates. If your profit margins are low, it may not be feasible to offer a commission that will be attractive enough for affiliates. For example, in my e-commerce marketplace business, we offer a $50 affiliate fee paid to the affiliate when they sign someone up for our VIP 12-month plan using their affiliate link. So realistically, if you are a VIP member yourself, you could get your money back in affiliate fees if you sign enough businesses up.

There are people who have affiliate marketing as one of their biggest income streams and literally make money selling other people's programs and services, taking a cut of each sale down through their affiliate link.

Affiliate program steps

- Choose an affiliate management platform. There are many platforms available that can help you manage your affiliate program, so do your research, read reviews on programs left from users, ask in Facebook groups what others use and make sure you know if you are paying for the use of the platform or if they are going to take a percentage of the transactions as well. On the marketplace, we use a free Plugin called SliceWP as my website is built on WordPress. It's okay, a little clumsy, but works well for the small number of affiliates we have. If we have hundreds in the future, we would need to look at a different program for sure. Do your research and choose one that fits your needs and budget.
- Make sure the affiliate management program can easily track sales and commission due – this has to be easy for you and for them to know where they are at and what income has been earned.
- Decide on the commission rate you will offer affiliates for each sale they generate. Make sure the commission is attractive enough to incentivise affiliates to promote your products or services but it's not so much that it cuts too much into your bottom line and makes having the affiliate program unprofitable.

> **BONUS TIP**
>
> If you decide to implement an affiliate program, make it simple for your affiliates to get sales for you. Create a marketing affiliate kit for them. The kit would have banners, text links, and other promotional materials that they can use to promote your products or services on their websites or social media channels. These should be eye-catching and include clear calls to action. Making it simple will make more sales for both you and them – so win/win.

How do you recruit affiliates? Reach out to your community, including purchasers of your product or services – they already love the product because they purchased it. Put ads into Facebook groups and mention the Affiliate program on your socials and website often – about once a month or more, depending on how important it is to you and your bottom line. You can also find potential affiliates through affiliate networks or by reaching out directly to bloggers or influencers in your industry.

Flipping sides for a moment, think about how you could earn money from Affiliate programs. Do some research for any programs you use daily or weekly in your business and see if they have an affiliate program you could use. I promote my Flodesk affiliate link often. I currently use Flodesk as an email marketing program and I really love it so have no trouble recommending it to others. It costs me $19US a month for the program and I get $19US for every affiliate I sign up. Potentially I could get my email program for free, if I get 12 people to sign up a year via my affiliate link – how cool is that? Take a look at the money you are leaving on the table via affiliate marketing.

Thought leadership in writing a book

This is a great marketing tactic. This – what I'm doing right this very second – writing a book. And if you are rolling your eyes and thinking, "Jenn, get out of town, I'll never write a book", my reply to you, my friend, is never say never because here I am doing it. And I'm nothing special. Just a girl who has a lot to say about marketing and felt the need to write it all down to help country small business owners, just like you. I'd written a 7,500-word chapter for a book before, but never one authored solely by myself.

Undertaking the writing of a book is definitely hard on the scale of harder marketing things to do. Why would you write a book? I guess for all the reasons you do most of your marketing. To be the go-to person in your industry, to set yourself apart from your competitors, to be the expert, to make sales, to build community, to get more leads, to diversify your income – and the list goes on.

This book is the first book I've written, so I am not an expert on this as a marketing activity. And to be honest, as I am writing this section of the book, it's not even done yet, so I don't know exactly how my book writing will pan out as far as a marketing strategy goes. But I have seen a lot of friends and colleagues move the needle in their business enormously by writing, publishing and marketing a book.

How do you know if writing a book is for you? If you have enormous amounts of content already in your business, your book is half written already, it's just not in book format yet. (We are talking about writing business books here, not fiction.) I have been blogging for over 10 years through three different businesses, I have been podcasting weekly for more than five years – so my content library looks like an actual library – it is huge. So writing this book, pulling content from blogs, podcasts, articles and my brain, seemed like the next natural thing to do. If you are like me and you are producing content on your subject matter expertise week in, week out, then I would say, book writing is for you.

And if you're not producing content or have a library of content? Book writing is still for you – the process will just look different. If you are keen to write a book, start by gathering information, putting down a liquid plan (I said liquid because it will chop and change and be added to and subtracted from), start putting time aside to write and consider getting yourself along to an author's retreat – that's what gave me the confidence to start. Sitting in a room full of authors-to-be, with four glorious days of thinking about writing a book. The author retreat I attended was run by Andrew Griffiths, so check him out – https://www.andrewgriffiths.com.au/.

What I have loved the most about writing this book is that I don't need to write in order, and definitely have not written in order. I have chosen the part I wanted to write on a particular day and just started. If I finished on page 11, I could start on page 101 next time – it didn't matter. I had a structure; I had my contents page and I just started where it felt right on the day. It's a luxury I know lots of authors don't have, but with a well-constructed contents page and plan, it might be possible for you too.

Never thought about writing a book? Never say never, my book-reading friend.

Produce a lead magnet

What's a lead magnet? A lead magnet is a piece of content created, for free, that you give away for the purpose of gathering contact details, mostly an email address. The lead magnet has a compelling reason for a prospect to connect with your brand or business and delivers value to them.

The lead magnet should be a free piece of content, but something people would be willing to pay for – as it has to be that GOOD. A lead magnet is often a PDF downloadable document, but it doesn't have to be – there are lots of ways you can create a lead magnet. In fact, I have a little sheet for you that's got 69 of them – 69 Irresistible Lead Magnet Ideas and funnily enough, you don't need to give your email address for it – just click the link and up it will come. If you want to see the list of 69 Irresistible Lead Magnet Ideas go to https://socialmediaandmarketing.com.au/magnetideas. (Also scan the QR code at the back of the book for a clickable link.)

The steps to create a lead magnet for your business

- **Step One:** Identify WHO your lead magnet is for.
- **Step Two:** Identify the ONE problem you want to solve.
  The important word here is ONE – you aren't solving war and peace, just one problem. What is the biggest issue, headache or challenge your prospective buyer is looking for help to solve?
- **Step Three:** Give your lead magnet a name, a compelling title.

- **Step Four:** Choose your format – remember I gave you a link to 69 of them before.
- **Step Five:** Create the lead magnet.
- **Step Six:** Put it out to the world and market it to your audience and get them to sign up for it.

Lead magnets are the most successful way I have built my email list. My best lead magnet has been my 108 Social Media Content Creation Ideas – you can download that by going to www.108social.com.au if you haven't got it already.

I have produced many lead magnets over my time as a small business owner. When I had my kitchenware retail store, we produced three recipe books as lead magnets a year. We also produced a lead magnet that helped our customers decide on which cookware to purchase, because that was one of the biggest challenges we heard from our customers every day. That lead magnet talked customers through exactly how to choose the perfect cookware for their needs. Now in my marketing business, I have lead magnets that cover my clients' challenges such as how to use Instagram, how to create Facebook ads that work, how to create a business plan or marketing plan, how to produce a lead magnet and much more. All ideas stemming from listening to my clients' biggest challenges and concerns in business.

> **CHALLENGE**
> Start thinking about what your lead magnet could be. Start brainstorming what your customers' biggest challenges are and then think about how you can solve that by producing a lead magnet.

Visual data storytelling with infographics

Infographics, a type of visual marketing, can be used in a variety of marketing campaigns. You can use them to educate buyers about new products or services, as a dataset or to enhance the marketing content you want to share by adding an eye-catching visual element. Infographics are a great way to present complex information in a visually appealing and easy-to-understand format. They're different from a flashy video but just as effective, yet are often forgotten about as a marketing strategy.

Infographics statistics

From a reader's point of view:

- 90% of the information transmitted to the brain is visual. (Infographic World – https://infographicworld.com/)
- On average, people will remember 65% of the information they see in a visual. They will only remember 10% of the information that they hear. (Cognition – https://brainrules.net/vision/)
- Infographics are 30 times more likely to be read in their entirety than blog posts or news articles. (Digital Information World – https://www.digitalinformationworld.com/)
- 65% of buyers are visual learners – meaning they absorb the most information when they look at an image, graphic or video. (Pearson – https://www.pearson.com/en-au/)

The stats indicate that we need to use more of them in our marketing to make our points. To use them effectively, we need to think about the following points:

- **Your target audience** – it just keeps coming up, doesn't it! Knowing your WHO, your target audience, is so crucial in being successful in your marketing.
- **Your topic** – this could be a problem your customers face or a solution your business provides. This could be something you talk about a lot in business but haven't expressed visually. Putting that information into an infographic simply helps explain the same thing in a different way – perhaps appealing to your more "visual" buyers.
- **Gathering data to support your message** – this could be data from your own business or industry research.
- **Designing your infographic** – keep in mind that it should be visually appealing, easy to read, and on-brand with your business, using your business tone and visual assets such as colours and fonts.

Infographics can be a powerful marketing strategy and by presenting information in a visually appealing and easy-to-understand format, you can engage your target audience and promote your business in a memorable way.

Do some research on what infographics you might be able to produce as part of your content marketing strategy to help your audience understand things a little more easily. You can do some research on Canva, Pinterest or Google.

Publish a magazine or catalogue

You could produce either a digital or print magazine or a catalogue for your business as a marketing strategy. Print magazines are definitely making a comeback, as discussed in Chapter 3. Catalogues, used appropriately, are great for making sales inside your business. Living on a rural farm, I see very few catalogues delivered and have to raid my Mum's stash when I go to visit. I especially love them at Christmas time.

Let's chat about producing a magazine first. This is certainly a harder marketing strategy to do as the effort and energy alone is huge, and whether you produce it digitally or do a print run, there's a cost involved, there's the whole design element, finding a printer, finding writers to write the articles and photographers to take the photos, proofreaders, editors, and the list goes on. But think about what producing a high-quality magazine says about your brand, about your business? Does it set you apart from your competitors? Absolutely. Does it make you a leading authority in your network and field? For sure. Producing a magazine is no different from any other marketing strategy I have talked about in this book – it needs to fit with your brand, ethos, overall marketing strategy and also produce either quality leads or put money in your bank (make you sales).

Producing a magazine could be a great way to showcase your products or services and establish yourself as a thought leader in your industry or it could be a great way of bringing your community together by showcasing their products and services. Maybe it's a great collaboration or partnership marketing strategy that you lead and can get you in front of a whole new audience filled with your ideal clients.

With regard to producing catalogues, this tip applies mainly to retailers. When I'm wondering whether many marketing strategies would work for my small business, I often look to the big end of town and see what the businesses with huge marketing budgets and lots of human power in employees are doing. The one thing many big stores continue to do is produce catalogues – printed ones. The big stores even ramp up frequency and production coming into the busy Christmas/summer buying season – another sign that this marketing strategy still works.

Obviously, we can't compete with weekly produced catalogues, (most of us would go broke trying), but producing one or two a year in peak buying seasons might make great sense. Back in my retail days, there was a buying group within our 200-odd-kilometre radius that sold similar products and they would get together and use their buying power to buy products from suppliers and then produce a catalogue, launched around Christmas time, with all their gorgeous gift ideas. We were never allowed into this group. One retailer thought she owned our territory, despite being 50 kms from my store, and wouldn't allow us in that group. It hurt. It hurt a lot but rather than getting angry, I got even. I produced our own Christmas Gift Guide, and you know what? Ours was so much better. We had total control over what products went into the catalogue, as well as the prices. It was a resounding success with locals everywhere bringing in our catalogue with their gift ideas circled, ready to buy.

Could you produce a catalogue for your products, even if just once or twice a year? Do you think that would have a positive impact on your sales numbers? Our local newspaper designed and printed our catalogue. Some were distributed through the local paper, some via email, some via snail mail and some by catalogue walkers, straight into mailboxes.

The year we produced our first Christmas catalogue, we almost doubled our sales from the same time the previous year. The flow-on effect for the rest of the year, with all those new people spending money in our store and our loyal customers increasing their average order value, ensured financial and profitable growth of our retail business, year on year.

This strategy did take an investment of time to produce and research, and was an expense to the business. You really do need to know your numbers and set goals around the expected return, before undertaking a marketing strategy like this one. But it's totally worth it.

Gratitude marketing – thank-you cards and Christmas cards

People always like to be thanked, and your customers are no different. Depending on the size of your business, sending cards on occasion might be an enormous job or a simple job. And why would you do it? To create a community, to create loyalty and to say thank-you – to make your customer or client feel like they matter, that they are important to you. In Tip #9, I told you why 68% of customers leave your business because they believe you don't care if they shop with you or not. How can you show them you definitely care? Send them a thank-you or Christmas card. No-one gets snail mail these days and you hardly get any Christmas cards at all. Talk about stand out from the crowd and your competition – this is a winner.

Back when my customer base was a lot bigger, in a different business, I would employ my mum, from September, to start handwriting Christmas cards for my VIP customers. Just a few a day, so that when I was ready to post them in the first week of December, they would be ready to go. Now I write my own and often include a small gift. Unfortunately, postage normally costs more than what the gift is worth but that's the price of sending something snail mail.

Thank-you cards are great to send to customers, but also to people who refer business to you and to other people who help you in business – perhaps suppliers, other small business owners up the road, your accountant, the tyre business and so forth. There is a lot of positive collateral in handwriting and sending a simple thank-you card.

You could also send birthday cards or even anniversary cards. Wedding photographers and marriage celebrants can do this super easily. I have seen real estate agents use them to send out to past clients with a not-so-subtle message – let us know if you want to sell or buy again. Just remember, 68%!

Host a retreat – an immersive brand experience

Want a marketing strategy that builds stronger relationships and creates a real sense of community among your audience? One where you can share your knowledge and that of other experts, promote wellness of your audience and generate new business? Magic wand flicked – enter the host a retreat marketing strategy.

I'm not sure if it is the people I am hanging out with or if the world around me has changed, but I see loads of retreat options these days. Full disclosure, I do offer retreats in my business, so I am a little biased as to their greatness as a marketing strategy as well as a clear sales business strategy.

My retreats are a mixture of business, learning and relaxation (wellness), but other amazing people in my community run retreats around cake decorating, nursing, book writing, course creating, pure down-time relaxation and many more.

As mentioned above, retreats are a great way to build stronger relationships with your community. By spending time together in a relaxed and informal setting, you can get to know your customers or clients on a deeper level and build trust and loyalty. They create a real sense of community among your customers or clients. By bringing people together who share a common interest or goal, you can foster a sense of belonging and connection.

If your retreat is around offering education or training, it could involve workshops or classes on topics related to your business or industry, providing valuable knowledge and skills to your customers or clients. I bring in local experts as well, sometimes to share knowledge, tips and tricks, hold classes such as yoga, but other times just to tell their story as a small business owner and inspire others in the room.

Retreats aren't only about mindfulness, yoga or other wellness activities, but they can be and these activities definitely help promote health and wellbeing among your community.

Running a retreat can also be a way to generate new business. By offering a unique and memorable experience, you may attract new customers or clients who are interested in your products or services. In fact, 50% of the people who come along to my retreats have never purchased from me before. They are obviously in my community, lurking, so to speak, but haven't worked directly with me or purchased a product or service before purchasing their ticket to come along to my retreat.

Overall, running a retreat can be a powerful way to connect with your community and create a positive impact on the people inside your community.

Digital store fronts – Google ads/Google Shopping ads

The dynamic realm of Google ads and Google Shopping ads – these powerful tools can supercharge your marketing strategy, boost your brand visibility and drive valuable sales. If you are in retail or have an e-commerce business, then this is definitely a tip for you. (It's not just for product-based businesses, but those businesses do see great success in getting to a different consumer audience through these paid strategies.)

So, what's the difference between a Google ad and a Google Shopping ad? Picture this: your potential customers are actively searching for products or services you offer – Google ads ensures your business appears at the top of their search results. Google Shopping ads take it a step further, allowing you to display images and prices of your products directly in search results. These ads stand out, attracting more clicks and higher conversion rates.

Google ads and Google Shopping ads rules

There are rules around getting a profitable return on investment into ads:

- Set clear goals before diving in, define your objectives. Are you aiming to increase website traffic, generate leads or drive direct sales?
- Identify the keywords or key phrases potential customers might use when searching for products like yours. Use Google's

Keyword Planner to discover relevant keywords and estimate their search volume.

- Obviously creating compelling ad copy helps. Writing captivating ad headlines and descriptions that address your customer's pain points and highlight your unique selling points, while keeping it concise, relevant and actionable all helps.
- Choose the right keywords and opt for a mix of broad, phrase and exact match keywords to reach a wider audience while maintaining precision.
- Send your ad leads to a dedicated landing page that aligns with the ad's content. A seamless user experience boosts conversion.

So far as Google Shopping ads go, here are some thoughts on making those successful and profitable too:

- Creating a product feed is the backbone of any Google Shopping ad campaign. A product feed is a structured list of your products, including titles, descriptions, prices and images. Make sure you keep it up to date and accurate.
- Use clear, concise and keyword-rich product titles and descriptions. Highlight key features and benefits to entice potential buyers.
- Use professional images that showcase your products from various angles. Clear and attractive images can significantly impact click-through rates. Remember your customer can't pick it up or try it on while Google shopping, so make sure you have loads of different photos showcasing your product.

Paid Google ads and Google Shopping ads are hard to do first go, but they do definitely get easier if you watch them, tinker with them and take time to read the results – even mid-campaign. Some tips for a successful campaign:

- Start small.
- Prioritise monitoring and adjusting your campaign's performance.
- Identify irrelevant keywords that trigger your ads and add them as negative keywords. This prevents wasted clicks and improves your ROI.

- With a significant portion of searches happening on mobile devices, ensure your ads and landing pages are mobile-friendly for a seamless experience.

Avoid these pitfalls:

- Ignoring data – please don't ignore the data. Don't rely on assumptions. Base your decisions on actual performance data – that's the beauty of digital marketing after all.
- Google rewards relevant and engaging ads with lower costs and better ad placements. Focus on improving your quality score over time.
- Definitely keep an eye on your competitors' strategies.

Remember, success in the world of online advertising takes time and experimentation. Be patient, open to learning and ready to adapt. Google ads and Google Shopping ads can become invaluable tools in your marketing arsenal, driving consistent growth for your small business. If you want to learn more, head to YouTube and watch some Google ads for beginners videos and be open to learning new things.

***

So that's that, a list of 18 marketing strategies or ideas that are a little harder to do. A little more "out of the box thinking" and they definitely require more effort, energy and sometimes resources than posting on social media once a week.

These ideas might not be for beginners. A small business is just starting out. But no matter where you are on your journey in business, don't discount them. I have run several retreats now, and 10 years ago I would have thought that I could never pull off a retreat. Seemed like a lot of work, I didn't think my community would want to pay me to come along and I didn't think I was the right person to host such an event. But alas, I was wrong on all counts! Maybe starting a podcast is too big right now for you, but being a guest isn't so hard? Maybe the idea of finding time to become a consistent blogger seems overwhelming, but writing 4 or 5 posts in 12 months for someone else and repurposing them seems doable? Whatever it is that has inspired you in this chapter, give it a go. Or if the timing is off, never say never – it might be just the strategy you are looking for in 6, 12 or 18 months' time.

Nothing changes if nothing changes, so be prepared to step outside your marketing comfort zone and do things that might make you uncomfortable but also might make you more profitable. That, my friend, is the name of the business game.

Chapter 7

THE POWER OF EMAIL MARKETING

The harder I work
the luckier I get.

—

**Julie Preer, Airtree Resort,
Yarrawonga, Victoria**

f I had to choose one, just one, section of marketing that I loved, this would be it. I am not sure where my love for email marketing comes from, but I am very partial to a fabulous email marketing sequence. Actually, I lie, I think it comes from when I had my retail business and we created and sent an email every week. It took us a long time to get the formula for the weekly newsletter email right, but when we did it was fabulously profitable. I loved doing the research for the weekly newsletters, I loved the feedback and the sense of community it created.

Email marketing

The biggest piece of feedback I get when it comes to email marketing is "but I hate emails", which means "I hate getting them, so why would I send them?" I have two responses – (a) you are not your own ideal client and (b) you only hate getting bad ones. I am sure there are emails you open every time because you love to read that particular one. True? List building, building your email list, is something you should do from today if you aren't already. Most business owners who "get" email marketing say they wish they'd started building their list earlier – do be like them, start today!

I can say hand on heart that the number one thing I recommend for small businesses who are looking to create impact in their marketing, is this – LIST BUILDING (also known as email marketing). I firmly believe it is a cornerstone of the growth and success of a business. Too many business owners are putting all of their marketing eggs in the one social media basket. If you're spending more time on social media than you are on developing email campaigns for your list, you are leaving money on the table!

Yes, I know that the glamour and excitement of social media is a drawcard, but email marketing can do so much heavy lifting in your business. Not only has it been around longer (a wider spread of your demographic is familiar with it), but email marketing can accurately nail one of the most important aspects of customer relationships – humans

"

The number one reason list building is so important is this: you don't own your following on social media and you don't own the space you occupy on the social media platform!

"

interacting with humans! Don't get me wrong, social media can be awesome for gaining exposure to new customers or clients. But email marketing can really hone in on creating a nurturing, sustainable relationship with that person. The number one reason you should be on social media is to get people off social media on to your email list.

Do you have a client or customer list? If so, is building that list something you schedule into your daily goals?

If you answered NO to either of these questions, then read on! No matter if you're in retail or a service-based business, list building should be a priority. I have seen firsthand how much a well-engaged list can bring to your business. While there are a tonne of experts out there talking about social media as a priority with engagement, content, connections and leads, there are very few talking about list building.

The number one reason list building is so important is this: you don't own your following on social media and you don't own the space you occupy on the social media platform!

I'll repeat that so it really sinks in – you can spend time (and money) only developing and building a social media following, and it can all be taken away in an INSTANT by the platform. You are at the mercy of someone else by using their platform to engage with your clients.

Algorithms can change overnight in social media, and suddenly you don't reach the same people as you did the day before. Or – worse – your account can be shut down with no notice, and you lose it overnight. Or worse again you are hacked and now the hackers are acting as you to your audience, and no doubt doing damage to your brand and confusing your community. Unless, of course, you have an email list and you can email them to tell them you've been hacked and ask them to start following you over here.

A business owner at a seminar I was hosting gave this very poignant example: She explained she previously had 100,000 engaged followers, and her account was shut down by the platform with no warning, no recourse, no discussion – due to a very innocuous post about a sporting event with "who do you think will win?" However, the social platform deemed it as gambling (instead of an opinion/engagement post as she intended) and completely shut her account. It cost her her business – as she had never concentrated on list building, her whole audience disappeared overnight. She had no way of communicating with those followers to tell them what happened and what to do next.

So my only question to you is if social media disappeared tomorrow, would you still have a business?

Based on businesses that I have owned and worked in, the engaged email lists sell more – it's a simple fact! People on a business email list are FIFTEEN times more likely to buy from that business via the list, instead of via social media. And the biggest positive of an email list – you OWN this database! The email list can't be taken away from you. Of course, a person could unsubscribe, or not update their email address to a current one, but the bottom line is that the email list remains yours. A social media platform can take away your access to your customer base in an instant – poof, it's gone, and there is nothing you can do about it. However, having an email list or customer database means you are essentially building a fence around that tribe you have spent so much time and energy building.

The end goal with this? To get your online followers to give you an email address so they can become an offline email subscriber to your business!

You may be wondering, "Jenn, how do I get people from social media on to my email list?" Great question, so glad you asked! We'll look at three ways to do this in the next tips.

Crafting effective opt-in forms

You want traffic that comes past your business online to have an easy way to give you their details. A basic form on your website, blog or email signature is a super easy process.

Making it simple for potential customers to opt in for information means you can then send them updates, a newsletter, blog links or relevant engaging content. In my previous retail kitchenware business, we consistently sent out newsletters that had engaging content, including interesting recipes and cooking tips. We had such great feedback, and people often commented that they looked forward to reading our emails as they always found something useful in them!

If you have an opt-in form, make sure it is in a prominent location and make sure it is right in front of your traffic – it can be a pop-up on your website, a header on your blog, part of your Instagram bio, an invitation via Facebook, you could do a giveaway, or make it an exit pop-up on your website. Be bold – put this where people will see it.

Running engaging and rewarding competitions

Competitions can be one of the quickest and easiest ways to grow your email list. You've just got to make sure you are growing it with qualified leads, as you want those people who not only want to win the prize, but are potential customers or clients who will engage with you. Really think about the prize, because it matters. I've seen so many bad examples of competitions because the prize is fabulous but has nothing to do with the business running the competition. See Tip #77 for more ideas and thoughts around running competitions.

While there may be a cost involved with running a competition or giveaway, the benefits of intentionally collecting the right leads coming into your business will help you drive more profits into your business. It will also help to grow your email list the right way and increase your reach to your customer or client base.

BONUS TIP

If you are running a contest or competition, make a specific landing page for this. Don't make it hard for your audience to know what to do next. Have a specific link or landing that they use to opt in – the easier it is, the more people will opt in. Also, if you are using a social media platform to run the competition, make sure you are up to date on the CURRENT rules the platform has to run the comp, as you can be blocked or banned for breaching them. You will also have to check you are complying with any applicable government regulations or laws so that you don't run into any issues there.

Offering freebies, downloads and guides

Create something of interest so that your audience will give you their email address in exchange for that freebie! Giving away free, valuable content is the number one way I grow my email list. My monthly Social Media Prompt Calendars have a social media prompt idea for every day of the month and are very popular, as is my freebie that's 108 Social Media Content Creation Ideas – it has been downloaded thousands of times. Creating freebies also gives me some intel into what people are looking for and the problems I can solve for them.

Your freebie doesn't have to be complicated or super pretty, they don't have to be professionally designed or overthought. You just need to deliver value and good content in in a clear way. My biggest goal, once people have downloaded something, is that they start implementing it. Because once they see I'm an expert in a particular area, they will become raving fans, and more ready to jump onto a paid offer I release in the future.

If you are interested in seeing this process in play, then go to the homepage on my website here: https://socialmediaandmarketing. com.au. When you scroll down you will see I have a great list of freebies on offer, and there is also a freebies link in the menu! If you haven't already, download the 108 Social Media Content Creation Ideas booklet. You can download my other freebies too – and thousands of people have done this (yep, so cool!).

If you haven't ever thought about doing a freebie before, definitely download one of mine. Observe the process and watch how someone else does something that you want to do in your business. If you go through the steps to download the freebie on my site, you can see how my process works and you may be able to apply this to your business. You'll see that I have a couple of extra steps in the process that are a series of calls-to-action before you receive the actual download – see how it plays out!

Once you have downloaded and engaged in the process, then use this to brainstorm your own freebie or lead magnet. Ask yourself – what can you give away to your audience so that they will give you their email address? What is the biggest problem you can solve for your audience? Don't overthink it, just start brainstorming. Want some idea magnet idea suggestions? Go here: https://bit.ly/69leadmagnetideas.

But for those of you who already have a list built, don't think you can get away from this chapter scot-free. There is ALWAYS room for improvement. Ask yourself these questions:

- How can I improve my list and make my list better?
- What value can I provide to my audience?
- How can I attract better or more qualified people to my list?
- How can I serve them even better?

If you already have a freebie or lead magnet, then start brainstorming on what your NEXT one could be. I can guarantee you that one lead magnet is not enough – you need to have lots of them over the course of your business. You may not release them all at once, but having a bank of lead magnets makes it easier for you to repurpose content and build it going forward to release it when the time is right. However, you don't need to create these all right now, but look to develop these going forward over a period of time. As always, there is next-level stuff you can do even if you already have an email list, to build your list and make your list (and what you offer) even better and more engaging.

How to write emails that get opened and read

Alrighty, I hope I have convinced you to start list building and the power of doing so. But once you have a list of people to nurture, how do you create emails that get opened and read? Well, let's dive into some tips on how you can do that.

But first, let's imagine a little scenario that will likely be familiar to anyone in business who has an email list.

You've carefully crafted an email.

You've laboured over each paragraph.

You've spent hours on the subject line (because we know just HOW important that is).

You hit send with an exhilarated sigh of relief. TICK!

But when you look at your email stats, some disappointment sets in.

You notice that the opens aren't as good as you'd hoped and the click-through numbers are low. I get it – this can be very disheartening when you put so much time and effort into crafting an email for your audience. You will then ask the following questions:

- What went wrong?
- And (more importantly), what can you do to fix it?
- How do I create emails that people look forward to?

Well, there are a couple of essential steps you need to follow to begin.

The first critical step is to look at the tone of your emails. If you want to get your emails read, it starts with writing to them like you are writing to a friend. Everyone loves to hear from a friend. Why? Because we're interested in what our friends are up to, we trust them, and are far more likely to consume what they send us. When drafting an email to go out to your list, it's crucial that you write like you are talking to ONE person. One person who you know intimately.

If you have a reasonable size list (or once your list grows) it's unlikely that you will personally know everyone on it. But, in fact, you really do know them – you know:

- what keeps them up at night
- their struggles
- how they tick
- how to help them reach their goal.

That's why when you write to them, you do it like you're writing to just one person – not a whole list.

Remember, the person you are writing to is someone who connected to you for a reason; they are your friend and they want you to speak to them that way.

12 tips to produce emails which will be opened

Here is my list of 12 awesome tips that will help you to produce emails people love to receive, love to read and perhaps even love to pass onto another person who'd get some joy or information from them too.

1. Only email when you can add value. Be helpful. Be generous. If you continuously send emails with no value, you will burn your list out. Remember, the line between welcome guest and annoying pest can be a fine one.

2. Have your actual name as your "from address". Not admin@ or info@. Make it personal – put your name to it. Your list is building a relationship with you, so it's important that the emails you send come from you, a source they can trust and recognise.

3. Personalisation of emails is a great idea because a person's name is a powerful rapport builder. But don't repeat a person's name too often – that just gets creepy!

4. Reward people for taking the time to read your email, maybe with an offer or awesome value or otherwise, simply inspire them. If you want to test how many of your emails are read, try slipping a special bonus in the copy towards the bottom – this can be a great indicator of just how closely your content is being read.

5. This is my favourite and I think the most critical to email success – make your subject line awesome. If people know specifically what they'll learn or how exactly you'll make them happier, more informed or better at business, they'll be itching to read what you've sent them. Take your time to generate a great subject line. Break it up! If you want to maintain someone's attention, don't use only words – use a number. Because digits, like 4 or 37, will help stop wandering eyes and maintain attention. Don't try and be too cute in your subject line. Quit cleverness. Simple, specific subject lines beat clever alternatives every time. Marketing is a test and measure activity, and your emails are no different. Experiment with using emojis in your headline – like numbers, they are a fantastic way to capture scrolling eyes!

6. Learn from the masters. Subscribe to excellent email lists and take note of their subject lines carefully. You're guaranteed to learn something. BONUS TIP: Keep track of emails you receive where the headline really grabs you – this way you can have an inspiration bank for when you send your emails out.

7. When it comes to email marketing, less is more. Keep it short. Long and unwieldy emails kill interest. Challenge yourself to keep it as concise and impactful as possible.

8. Don't be afraid to mix up your greetings. Try Hi, Hey, Happy Monday, Hey (name), Dear Awesome (target market), or Greetings from Sunny Mulwala! Mixing up your greetings makes you less robotic and more personal.

9. Develop a brand and a brand voice. Consider your emails to be a way of talking to your customers or readers as your new FRIENDS. Be consistent in the tone and topics you cover so you avoid wandering off-brand.

10. Add personality. Use (proprietary language) words or expressions only you use – this makes up a big part of your brand voice. But at the same time, be human and don't drown people in confusing acronyms.

11. Write short paragraphs and be succinct. Use CAPITALS or **bold** or <u>underline</u> to draw the reading eye to certain parts of the email, because we all skim these days – especially if there are big long paragraphs.

12. Segment your list where you can. Segmenting your list is how you continue to make your list powerful. Sending a really curated email to a specific section of your email list enhances the relationship you are nurturing. For example, running an event in Wagga Wagga? Being able to segment your list to just those who live in the Riverina plus 100 kilometres is marketing magic. Sending that email to everyone on your list will cause the person in Queensland to roll their eyes and think, really – why send this to me? Or sending an email to your past customers who've purchased products for their dogs or love Australian made products makes it more relevant to them and makes them feel like you really do know them and care. Segmenting your list is critical. Do it from the start, as much as you can.

The harsh truth about emails is that everyone's inbox is overflowing. Nobody is desperate to receive more emails. You should be honoured that people have opted into your list and are happy to receive your emails. Each subscriber has given you a hard-earned vote of confidence. But be careful. Never take anyone's attention for granted. Because everyone's time is precious. Week in and week out, you have to prove your value to your email subscribers. Know your readers so well that you can empathise with their struggles. Ask questions – and offer help.

Write as if you're emailing one good friend because that's how people will get to know you, like you and trust you. When you've earned those three things, you've earned the ability to push send and grow your business.

To finish out this chapter on my favourite marketing strategy, email marketing, let's cover three basic questions:

1. **How often should you email your list?** I refer you back to Tip #103 – the fine line between guest and pest. Weekly is great (possibly bi-weekly if you are in retail), fortnightly is good too and monthly is okay. Quarterly is getting lazy and random emails are never going to help build your business. You are an expert at what you do, otherwise, you would not be in business. You do have enough knowledge to email your list monthly, at the very least. Any less than this and your audience will probably forget about you and you won't be top of mind for them.

2. **What email marketing system should I use?** Gosh, this is a tough one because this book will probably outlast any advice I give here. The best advice is do some research and don't just go with free. Free email marketing platforms or free beginner packages often result in bad deliverability – your email doesn't get delivered. Remember the golden rule of free – if it's free, then you're the product. Klaviyo is brilliant for e-commerce businesses, and I personally love Flodesk – you can get my exclusive deal with Flodesk here: https://flodesk.com/c/LOVEJENN

3. **What do I email them?** This is a question that can only be answered by knowing your specific business. Email them what you think they would like to know. Remember my emails in my retail

business? Well, our formula for the weekly emails was always the same. Three things – a product, a recipe and a cooking tip (we were a kitchenware shop). But we got smart as time moved on and either the recipe or the cooking tip related to the product. So really, we were selling without selling in the eyes of our reader. And although you probably can't use the same formula for your emails, I am sure you can come up with your own. If you want to know what your customers or clients want to know do some research in Facebook groups, ask ChatGPT or Google, head over to Quora and join some forums, take a look at Reddit or Google Trends or do some research over on Pinterest.

Emails don't have to be war and peace – they just have to be engaging.

***

If you're not already building your list or emailing your audience/community, then this is the biggest nudge I can give you to start because there's every chance your competitors are in their inbox nurturing your customers.

If you still need convincing, here's some data of social media versus email marketing:

- The average open rate for marketing emails across industries is around 21.33%, while the average click-through rate is about 2.62%. In comparison, the average engagement rate on Facebook is around 0.17%.
- Email marketing tends to have higher conversion rates than social media. The average conversion rate for email campaigns is approximately 4.29%, while the average conversion rate for social media is around 0.59%.
- Email marketing consistently delivers a higher ROI compared to social media marketing. According to a survey by DMA, the average ROI for email marketing is $42 for every $1 spent, while social media has an average ROI of $17 for every $1 spent.

- According to a survey conducted by MarketingSherpa, 72% of consumers prefer to receive promotional content through email, compared to 17% who prefer social media. This statistic indicates that email is a preferred channel for receiving promotional messages and suggests that consumers are more receptive to marketing communications in their inbox.

Boom – that's it – that is me done convincing you that email marketing is the way to go and hopefully you'll love it as much as I do because your bank balance is growing.

THE FUTURE OF MARKETING

I f you live under a rock you probably haven't heard of AI – not AL as one of my friends thought once – but AI (Artificial Intelligence), and not artificial insemination as farmers might think!

In recent years we have seen the rise and rise of more AI from Apple's Siri (2011) to face recognition on our smart phones and algorithms used by social media platforms. I would go so far to say that we don't actually realise just how much AI we use in our everyday lives – we just use it without thinking about the fact that it's artificial intelligence. It's easy to dismiss because it makes our lives simpler and easier and we always love a product that can do that.

In late 2022 ChatGPT was introduced to the public, although much of the world didn't embrace it until early 2023. Now many of us (myself included) use it almost daily in our businesses. So, this begs the question, where will the likes of ChatGPT and other conversational AI models lead us in the future and what will our marketing look like as small business owners in the country?

I think that AI is just part of the digital revolution we are going through. Just like hunters and gathers had to embrace the agricultural revolution and then the industrial revolution where things moved from mostly agricultural to the makings of our modern society, this too is part of an evolution.

Like the Instagramers who embraced reels first and built their following to large numbers and then made bucket loads of money teaching everyone else how to build their following using reels, those who embrace AI in their marketing will be the winners. People who are early adopters and tech enthusiasts will be the winners in business. It's always been the way – early adopters are rewarded.

So, AI is not to be feared and I would one thousand percent encourage you to embrace it and be an early adaptor. It will not only change the way you market your products and services, but it is also going to change the way you interact with your customers and clients. Even ChatGPT believes in its own future, because if you ask it about itself, it will tell you that it has become an invaluable tool for businesses – so it can't be wrong, right?

But AI isn't just about ChatGPT, it's also about algorithms in our favourite social media platforms using data to serve us up things it believes we are interested in, and therefore doing the same to your customers and clients. It's about Chatbots that help you automate and optimise various business practices like emails, website enquiries and more.

AI will help us deliver hyper-personalised experiences to our customers, by analysing vast amounts of customer data which us humans would struggle to match. We can then use this to tailor our marketing campaigns, offers and recommendations to suit the individual preferences of our amazing community. All this will help with building better communities and therefore, long-lasting relationships. Being able to use data to make strategic decisions in business is one of the reasons I love digital marketing so much – having AI to help me discover those strategic decisions will give me the competitive edge.

I do hope that AI will make marketing cheaper and more accessible to more small business owners. With so many small business owners caught in the trap of working "in" their business and not "on" their business, AI could be the answer to their "I need more time" prayers. Of course, making marketing more cost effective enables us to then compete with our more urban and city counterparts on a more even playing field. How can it potentially reduce costs? By having AI-powered marketing tools that can automate repetitive tasks, it will reduce labour costs and free up time.

But AI isn't the only thing happening in marketing at the moment. There's lots of other ways our marketing will change as we head into the future. The change is being driven by technology but also by us, as consumers.

Future marketing changes to watch

- Voice-activated searches – I'm not sure about you, but I'm always asking Google to switch on my TV or what the weather is going to be like today or to play this song or that movie or I'm asking Siri how to spell this word or that word (spelling is not my best attribute!). Voice-activated search is becoming more a part of our everyday lives and it's just a matter of time before we all tell a device what we want to order and have it arrive in time for dinner. So, what does that mean for your content and your marketing? If I asked Siri to recommend the best [insert your industry] in [insert your town name] – would your business name be one that's mentioned in the search results?

- Augmented Reality (AR) and Virtual Reality (VR) – this technology has some incredibly positive impacts on rural and regional areas, especially where services are limited – I am already doing telehealth with doctors online. Or maybe you are the clothing store and your customers are in the city, hours away, and want to buy from you – AR might be where you need to look for the future of your marketing. Similarly, VR will open up many more doors to any business that does real life or in person tours to now offer virtual tours, and bring in a whole new audience of buyers and a brand new income stream.

- Sustainability and social responsibility – the rise of the conscious consumer is already happening. A conscious consumer is a customer who demands sustainable and socially responsible products and services. Businesses embracing sustainable initiatives are already differentiating themselves by aligning their marketing efforts to their conscious consumer. Highlighting eco-friendly practices, supporting local causes or showcasing ethical sourcing can attract conscious consumers and foster loyalty.

- Video marketing dominance – anyone who doesn't embrace video will fall further behind as video content will continue to dominate the marketing landscape. Go back and read Tip #11 and, if necessary, step outside your comfort zone.

- Personal data privacy and consent – we saw the GDPR (EU general data protection regulation) introduced a few years back – it's the strongest privacy and security law in the world. As data privacy concerns grow, consumers are becoming more cautious about sharing personal information. Small businesses must prioritise data security and transparency in their marketing practices. It's essential to maintain customer trust and loyalty.

- Social media platforms will continue to evolve into powerful e-commerce channels creating seamless shopping experiences. Shopping features will be integrated directly into social media posts, which sort of happens now with the ability to tag a product in your Instagram or Facebook store. Social commerce will go one step further and the check-out will also be on the social platforms, as opposed to the check-out being on your website or a third-party site. Of all the predictions of marketing strategies, I have to say that this one scares me the most. Relying more and more on platforms we have little control over makes me nervous for the average small business owner.

- User-Generated Content (UGC) will continue to be a valuable asset for marketing efforts. User-Generated Content is basically – you sell me a dress, then I wear the dress, tagging your business in my photo of me wearing the dress, because I bought it from you, and then you, as the business owner, share my content as part of your brand awareness or selling strategy. If you aren't already leveraging UGC – then start today! Encourage your customers to create and share content related to your brand, such as reviews, testimonials or social media posts. By leveraging UGC, businesses can tap into the power of authentic recommendations and social proof, strengthening their brand reputation and attracting new customers.

- Messaging apps like WhatsApp, Facebook Messenger and WeChat are becoming popular channels for customer communication and marketing. You can leverage these platforms to engage with your customers and provide personalised recommendations. Many years back, when I was in retail, we'd send photos of a product to target customers, with a short message saying, "thought of you when

I saw this" or "this is SO you", encouraging them to come in to buy the product. Or again, we'd send customers voice messages or a photo to say your order has arrived – adding that personal touch to a simple message. Messaging apps take this level of personalised service to another level, if done right.

- Interactive content and gamification – these two are in their infancy and are just starting to enter our mainstream marketing, but mark my word, they will be huge. This depends, of course, on your target audience. But if your target audience is under 25 or into gaming, (any age), then using interactive content and gamification to capture and maintain your customers' attention can create memorable experiences. Interactive content and gamification can include quizzes, contests, interactive videos or augmented reality games. This is definitely a watch this space marketing strategy.

- Subscription-based and membership models will continue to thrive in the future. They aren't massive in Australia right now, especially subscription-based business models, but if the US is anything to go by, currently worth over US$28.1 billion, consumers are going to love them. Start to think outside the marketing box – what could you do as a subscription-based business?

But some things won't change, they will just get better with age. One of those things is us, the small business owner in the country, and our local customers, putting a greater emphasis in the future on supporting local businesses and connecting with our communities. Community and shopping local, supporting local, is a movement that was revitalised by businesses like my Buy From a Bush Business Facebook group and Buy From the Bush on Instagram, not to mention a global pandemic. We saw the value of supporting people in our own communities for ourselves and the future of our towns.

My marketing predictions above highlight the diverse opportunities that lie ahead for us here in the country. I even asked the future of marketing, AI, to weigh in on the prediction above. But it's up to us to continue to embrace innovation, stay connected with consumer trends and leverage technology to our advantage, so our businesses can position themselves for long-term success in the evolving marketing landscape.

FINAL THOUGHTS

So, you made it to the end. You've read 107 marketing tips and now we are here – almost at the end.

Or, you're exactly like me and you came here first. You read the last chapter first – just to make sure the book was worth reading in the first place – before you commit. If so, we are SO alike. Read the rest of the book – it is good, trust me.

The number one message I wanted you to get throughout reading this book was to *make marketing a priority*. No matter if you choose tip #7 or tip #107, make it a priority to implement, test, measure, fix, polish, re-implement until you reach success.

If you want to grow your business, you have to market. You cannot have a business without customers or clients, and you cannot have a successful business without making marketing a priority.

Whether you have to make an appointment with yourself each week to do your marketing, like I do to get my bookwork done, or whether you outsource your marketing to another expert, or whether you commit to 10 minutes a day – whatever works for you, as long as you do it. "It" being making marketing a priority.

You might be thinking, *Jenn, I get it, I need to make time for marketing*, to which I exhale with enthusiasm, but will you? Will you really? Will you put down this book and start marketing better or more?

Two of my favourite motivational quotes, both from my business mentor many years ago, are:

- Nothing changes if nothing changes.
- Ready. Fire. Aim.

Remember them both well. Literally nothing changes, if nothing changes. And if things are to change, it's up to you.

And Ready, Fire, Aim – the world doesn't need another small business owner in a country area "aiming" to do something. Your community needs, you need, the world needs more ACTION TAKERS – so be an action taker and that action is marketing your business.

READY, FIRE, AIM is about taking action NOW. You will never have success, happiness, financial security, better health, richer relationships or anything else that is important to you in the future unless you recognise you have to begin creating them RIGHT NOW.

The key message is don't *aim* to make the call, book a meeting, create a marketing piece – FIRE. Those brave enough to do so ultimately will win. Be willing to risk failure and temporary setbacks and to move in the direction of your goals with unwavering faith in your own abilities. Remember you are not trying to outperform anyone else but yourself. This is about being the best you can be. You are ready, now is your time so start firing.

You'll be amazed what you can achieve when you commit to taking action (ahem, do more marketing) in a focused direction on a daily basis. However, I won't be amazed, I know how powerful marketing is and that's why I wrote this book that you've now finished.

You've got this, my friend. You've got this.

Want some more
Jenn Donovan
in your life?

If you've found amazing value in Jenn's latest book, there are several opportunities to collaborate and connect further with her. Explore the details on the following pages or visit:

www.jenndonovan.com.au

Make sure you join her community and connect with Jenn on Instagram, Facebook, LinkedIn and Threads, where she's always giving more and more marketing value.

Take your marketing to the next level – join the program

If this book helped you think about your marketing, strategy and business a little differently and helped you make marketing a priority, why not sign up for Jenn's new program?

The 9 Week Marketing Transformation Program is a dynamic program tailored for small business owners aiming to quickly improve their marketing strategies and bounce back from business challenges.

Jenn's program is all about taking the knowledge you have learned from reading this book and transferring it in a practical way that empowers you to make marketing a priority. This highly practical program walks business owners step-by-step through how to design a marketing message that gets attention, create marketing that maximises their reach and community engagement, and reveals the most effective methods for your business, to amplify what you do and win more business!

If you'd like to know more about this 9 Week Marketing Transformation Program individually or as part of a group, please drop Jenn a line at **jenn@jenndonovan.com.au** or to find out more, scan the QR Code below.

Join Jenn's community

Join the Community! The inspiring rural and regional small business community online where you can find business owners, just like you, who have also read this book and are now marketing ACTION TAKERS. Join Jenn's Facebook group Like Minded Business Owners.

If there's one thing Jenn knows, it's about building community, and as she's travelled around the regions of Australia, she's seen more and more small business owners who just want to hang out with those people "who get it". They "get" what it's like to run a small business in rural and regional areas with all its peaks and troughs, booms and busts.

The world of small business has become more complex and complicated and although Jenn knows this book has some answers to your questions, perhaps you want more, need more? If that sounds like you, join the group!

Hang out, work through an issue you're having with the group, collaborate with other members, ask your burning questions, get support, practical knowledge, futuristic thinking, all the things you need when it comes to support in the small biz world.

Check out Like Minded Business Owners here: **https://bit.ly/LMBOJenn** or scan the QR code below – Your Community is waiting for you!

Not just another
"marketing" coach!

The world of small business moves quickly – since starting this book new social media platforms have been launched, new ways to use AI (artificial intelligence) have become daily habits, the algorithm has changed over a million billion times (I am guessing!) which disrupts how we market and a marketing strategy that I tested and measured eight months ago that flunked is now bringing in a three-fold ROI. This is why we have overwhelm in business – things move so quickly.

Jenn's not just another marketing coach because her approach is all about YOU. Where you are in business, where you want your goals to take you and what you need your marketing to do for you. No BS and certainly no cookie-cutter generic stuff – boo hiss.

Jenn works with a limited number of business owners to help them find their way with marketing, making it a priority, understanding their strategy and how to implement it and how to measure, tweak and polish it.

The bottom line is if you want a profitable and sustainable business you need a coach who's in the trenches, testing and measuring, watching for trends in the market, the economy and in people, and that's Jenn. Jenn helps you develop your marketing muscle to thrive in the modern business world. It's not about hustle culture, "bigger is better" or always looking for the next sale, it's about community, prioritising marketing, understanding your customer, setting goals and squishing all this into a strategy that works for YOU.

Want to know more about working with Jenn?
Email Jenn – **jenn@jenndonovan.com.au**.

www.jenndonovan.com.au

Need an engaging, influential and highly experienced speaker for your next live or virtual event?

Jenn Donovan has delivered hundreds of presentations, workshops (in real life and virtual), webinars, seminars and retreats over the past 10 years and has shared her wisdom around the country, in the city and even to international audiences.

Jenn possesses an impressive set of skills as both a captivating speaker and a joyous storyteller. Her engaging presentations leave audiences feeling inspired, motivated and ready to take decisive action. With over two decades of successful business ownership and her expertise as a marketing futurist, Jenn draws upon a wealth of experience and stays up to date with the latest trends and developments in our rapidly evolving business landscape.

What sets Jenn apart is her approachable and down-to-earth style of presenting. Her talks are filled with relatable stories, humour and humility, creating a genuine connection with her listeners. She genuinely cares about each audience member, ensuring they leave with a sense of inspiration and a practical list of actions to propel their businesses towards their desired goals. It's no surprise that Jenn has earned the title of BEST SPEAKER time and time again at various events, as she goes above and beyond to understand her audience and exceed their expectations for the day.

To find out more about getting Jenn to speak at your next event, either face to face or virtually, email **jenn@jenndonovan.com.au**.

www.jenndonovan.com.au

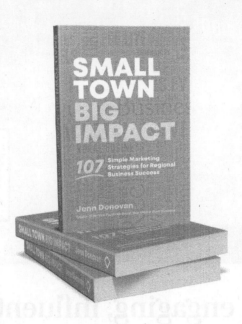

This book is the perfect gift for your small business customers

If you're looking for something a little different, a book that inspires and you just know your customers will appreciate, then Jenn would love to offer you the chance to buy this book in bulk to give as a gift.

Maybe you're looking for a thank-you gift, or want to send a client a gift to show you are there for them in business or maybe you've got an event coming up and need a gift for the audience?

This book is it. There's no other marketing book out there for small rural and regional business owners, so you can't go wrong!

Want to chat about what we can do together?

Reach out to Jenn – **jenn@jenndonovan.com.au** and let's chat. We could even do a special print run with a message just from you to your customers – now that would be cool.

www.jenndonovan.com.au

Would you like to interview Jenn Donovan?

Jenn is a well-seasoned podcaster with her own podcast *Small Business Made Simple*, ranking in the top 1.5% globally, so she's no stranger to the interview process – from either side of the mic. Jenn has been interviewed many times for other podcasts, radio, live TV and publication features.

Jenn can talk with great gusto on the following topics (but not limited to, of course!):

- The evolution of and future of business marketing
- How to Future Proof Your Business
- How to Build a Community to Build a Business
- How to be a Person of Influence
- Marketing to the Different Generations
- Human to Human (H2H) Marketing
- Data Driven Marketing
- Content Marketing
- Artificial Intelligence and Marketing Automation
- E-Commerce and Online Retail
- Plus many more topics in relation to Small Business and Small Business Marketing – get in touch.

If you'd like to interview Jenn about any of the above or her latest book, *Small Town Big Impact – 107 simple marketing strategies for regional business success*, please email Jenn at **jenn@jenndonovan.com.au**.

www.jenndonovan.com.au

Listen to Jenn's Podcast – *Small Business Made Simple*

Our time together doesn't have to end now you're at the end of the book. In fact, it might have just begun! Tune into the *Small Business Made Simple* podcast for weekly marketing and business chats with Jenn and her amazing expert guests.

Why tune in?

With **over half a decade** in the podcasting realm, I've interviewed the brightest minds, dissected the toughest challenges, and uncovered the hidden gems of the small business marketing world and I share it all in my weekly episodes.

Every episode is packed with Jenn-isms, actionable insights, marketing thoughts and ideas, and strategies that have been tried and tested.

With over **200,000 downloads** and ranked in the **top 1.5% globally**, make sure you join the thousands of weekly small business listeners.

Whether you're just starting out or looking to scale, there's something for you.

How to listen

Search for *Small Business Made Simple* on your favourite podcast platform like Apple or Spotify, and make sure you click "Subscribe" to ensure you never miss an episode. Of course, you can also listen to every episode by heading to my website www.socialmediaandmarketing.com.au/podcast.

Don't just read about marketing. Listen, learn, and lead your business to new heights!

What my listeners say:

> *"Relevant and so good! This is the best podcast I have listened to for business."* **McMinis**

> *"If you're in business listen to this podcast! I've started from the beginning. Incredibly valuable."* **Katie M, Wattle & Gum**

> *"Absolute best resource for a time-poor small business owner! Love the jingle too!"* **Jane, Ruby's Homestore**

Additional resources (with marketing love from Jenn)

Throughout the book I've mentioned some other great resources I would love to share with you to help you make marketing a priority and to continue our marketing journey together.

So, for all the extra resources, workbooks and freebies mentioned in the book (plus more), click the QR code below, choose your option and enjoy.

Scan here